W9-BFZ-505

THE WAVE

Man, God, and the Ballot Box
in the Middle East

HERBERT & JANE DWIGHT WORKING GROUP ON ISLAMISM AND THE INTERNATIONAL ORDER

THE WAVE

Man, God, and the Ballot Box in the Middle East

Reuel Marc Gerecht

HOOVER INSTITUTION PRESS

STANFORD UNIVERSITY | STANFORD, CALIFORNIA

www.hoover.org

Hoover Institution Press Publication No. 608

Hoover Institution at Leland Stanford Junior University, Stanford, California 94305-6010

First printing 2011

17 16 15 14 13 12 11   9 8 7 6 5 4 3 2 1

Manufactured in the United States of America

The paper used in this publication meets the minimum Requirements of the American National Standard for Information Sciences—Permanence of Paper for Printed Library Materials, ANSI/NISO Z39.48-1992. ⊗

Cataloging-in-Publication Data is available from the Library of Congress.
    ISBN 978-0-8179-1334-2 (cloth : alk. paper)
    ISBN 978-0-8179-1336-6 (e-book)

*The Hoover Institution gratefully acknowledges
the following individuals and foundations
for their significant support of the*

HERBERT AND JANE DWIGHT WORKING GROUP
ON ISLAMISM AND THE INTERNATIONAL ORDER:

Herbert and Jane Dwight
Stephen Bechtel Foundation
Lynde and Harry Bradley Foundation
Mr. and Mrs. Clayton W. Frye Jr.
Lakeside Foundation

For Max

CONTENTS

For decades, the themes of the Hoover Institution have re-
volved around the broad concerns of political and economic
and individual freedom. The cold war that engaged and challenged our nation during the twentieth century guided a good
deal of Hoover's work, including its archival accumulation
and research studies. The steady output of work on the communist world offers durable testimonies to that time, and
struggle. But there is no repose from history's exertions, and
no sooner had communism left the stage of history than a
huge challenge arose in the broad lands of the Islamic world.
A brief respite, and a meandering road, led from the fall of
the Berlin Wall on 11/9 in 1989 to 9/11. Hoover's newly
launched project, the Herbert and Jane Dwight Working
Group on Islamism and the International Order, is our contribution to a deeper understanding of the struggle in the
Islamic world between order and its nemesis, between Muslims keen to protect the rule of reason and the gains of modernity, and those determined to deny the Islamic world its
place in the modern international order of states. The United
States is deeply engaged, and dangerously exposed, in the Islamic world, and we see our working group as part and parcel
of the ongoing confrontation with the radical Islamists who

have declared war on the states in their midst, on American power and interests, and on the very order of the international state system.

The Islamists are doubtless a minority in the world of Islam. But they are a determined breed. Their world is the Islamic emirate, led by self-styled "emirs and mujahedeen in the path of God" and legitimized by the pursuit of the caliphate that collapsed with the end of the Ottoman Empire in 1924. These masters of terror and their foot soldiers have made it increasingly difficult to integrate the world of Islam into modernity. In the best of worlds, the entry of Muslims into modern culture and economics would have presented difficulties of no small consequence: the strictures on women, the legacy of humiliation and self-pity, the outdated educational systems, and an explosive demography that is forever at war with social and economic gains. But the borders these warriors of the faith have erected between Islam and "the other" are particularly forbidding. The lands of Islam were the lands of a crossroads civilization, trading routes, and mixed populations. The Islamists have waged war, and a brutally effective one it has to be conceded, against that civilizational inheritance. The leap into the modern world economy as attained by China and India in recent years will be virtually impossible in a culture that feeds off belligerent self-pity, and endlessly calls for wars of faith.

The war of ideas with radical Islamism is inescapably central to this Hoover endeavor. The strategic context of this clash, the landscape of that Greater Middle East, is the other pillar. We face three layers of danger in the heartland of the Islamic world: states that have succumbed to the sway of terrorists in which state authority no longer exists (Afghanistan, Somalia, and Yemen), dictatorial regimes that suppress their people at home and pursue deadly weapons of mass destruction and adventurism abroad (Iraq under Saddam Hussein, the Iranian theocracy), and "enabler" regimes, such as the ones in Egypt and Saudi Arabia, which export their own problems with radical Islamism to other parts of the Islamic world and beyond. In this context, the task of reversing Islamist radicalism and of reforming and strengthening the state across the entire Muslim world—the Middle East and Africa, as well as South, Southeast, and Central Asia—is the greatest strategic challenge of the twenty-first century. The essential starting point is detailed knowledge of our enemy.

Thus, the working group will draw on the intellectual resources of Hoover and Stanford and on an array of scholars and practitioners from elsewhere in the United States, the Middle East, and the broader world of Islam. The scholarship on contemporary Islam can now be read with discernment. A good deal of it, produced in the immediate aftermath of 9/11, was not particularly deep and did not stand the test of time and events. We, however, are in the favorable position of a "second generation" assessment of that Islamic material. Our scholars and experts can report, in a detailed, authoritative way, on Islam within the Arabian Peninsula, on trends within Egyptian Islam, on the struggle between the Kemalist secular tradition in Turkey and the new Islamists, particularly the fight for the loyalty of European Islam between these who accept the canon, and the discipline, of modernism and those who don't.

Arabs and Muslims need not be believers in American exceptionalism, but our hope is to engage them in this contest of ideas. We will not necessarily aim at producing primary scholarship, but such scholarship may materialize in that our participants are researchers who know their subjects intimately. We see our critical output as essays accessible to a broader audience, primers about matters that require explication, op-eds, writings that will become part of the public debate, and short, engaging books that can illuminate the choices and the struggles in modern Islam.

We see this endeavor as a faithful reflection of the values that animate a decent, moderate society. We know the travails of modern Islam, and this working group will be unsparing in depicting them. But we also know that the battle for modern Islam is not yet lost, that there are brave men and women fighting to retrieve their faith from the extremists. Some of our participants will themselves be intellectuals and public figures who have stood up to the pressure. The working group will be unapologetic about America's role in the Muslim world. A power that laid to waste religious tyranny in Afghanistan and despotism in Iraq, that came to the rescue of the Muslims in the Balkans when they appeared all but doomed, has given much to those burdened populations. We haven't always understood Islam and Muslims—hence this inquiry. But it is a given of the working group that the pursuit of modernity and human welfare, and of the rule of law and reason, in Islamic lands is the common ground between America and contemporary Islam.

REUEL MARC GERECHT knows both the classics of Islamic history and the life of Arab and Muslim streets. This book is born of that unique temperament and experience. A former case officer in the Central Intelligence Agency's Clandestine Service, Gerecht belongs to a long trail of illustrious intelligence officers, "spies," drawn to duty in distant lands. A line runs from T. E. Lawrence to Reuel Gerecht, Westerners who venture into Arab and Islamic lands and never really quit them. This kind of sensibility is special, and gives rise to works of intense engagement. We are richer for these works, because there runs in that genre of writing an eye for the intimacies, and twists and turns, of these societies. After immersion in the classics of Islam, and inspired by one of the greats of Islamic studies, the historian Bernard Lewis, Gerecht pursued his passion for the peoples and lands of Islam. The title of one of his previous books, *Know Thine Enemy: A Spy's Journey into Revolutionary Iran*, captures the man's drive and curiosity.

The Wave, in its title, pays tribute to the late Samuel P. Huntington, doubtless the best and most penetrating political scientist of the five or six decades now behind us. In *The Third Wave: Democratization in the Late Twentieth Century* (1991), Huntington captured modern democracy's trajectory, the "waves" that carried it to previously authoritarian settings, then the "reversals" in its fortunes as economic and political failures, and the temptations held out by demagogues and "strongmen," shattered the faith in democracy's appeal. Islamic societies have proven remarkably resistant to democracy's call, and Huntington wrote of this. With Huntington and Bernard Lewis as intellectual guides, Gerecht takes up that great question, democratic possibility in Islamic lands. He comes forth with a verdict of considerable power and originality. That "Third Wave" that proved so seminal in the triumph of democracy and its extraordinary advance that took place between 1974 and 1990, and remade East Asia and Latin America, could well be on its way to the domains of Islam. There is argument and vigor in this book, and that unique mix of learning and savvy that has given the work of "scouts" and "lookouts" their timeless appeal and power.

FOUAD AJAMI
Senior Fellow, Hoover Institution
Cochairman, Herbert and Jane Dwight Working Group
on Islamism and the International Order

ACKNOWLEDGMENTS

Although writing is a solitary profession, a book is a collective effort. *The Wave* would not have been born without the encouragement and criticism of others. I must first thank John Raisian and the Hoover Institution. Without their support, this book would still be wandering aimlessly in my mind. I need to give a special thanks to Oie Lian Yeh, an editor at Hoover Press, for her aesthetic eye and editing acumen. Her name in Chinese alludes to the beauty of water lilies, which seems most apposite given the elegance that she tried to bestow upon my prose. I need to thank Megan Ring of Hoover, who was always there helping with those things that, if left unattended, will stop the mind and the printing press. I need to also thank my former assistant at the American Enterprise Institute, Jeff Azarva, who provided invaluable help in researching the Muslim Brotherhood, about which he knows more than I. I must thank Cliff May and my other colleagues at the Foundation for Defense of Democracies, who have unfailingly supported me in my endeavors and put up with my considerable crankiness as I finished this book.

I have been thinking about the collision of modernity and Islam since I lived in Cairo—an exquisite mess of a metropolis—in 1980. My curiosity gained force several years later when I moved to Istanbul—the most captivating city of the Muslim world in great part because it sits on the most historic, and the most beautiful, fault line between Christianity and Islam. This book is part of my continuing rumination on what Bernard Lewis first called the "clash of civilizations."

I owe a large intellectual debt to my friend and former colleague Gary Schmitt, a resident scholar at the American Enterprise Institute. Although Gary is not a student of Islam, he's got one of the best minds I've ever met. He has drunk deeply of Western philosophy and politics. We have often discussed the themes of this book; he has regularly caused me to revisit what I thought I knew about Islamic and Occidental history. He has certainly shown me that even with the most modern subjects, all things start with Aristotle.

I am similarly indebted to the historian Robert Kagan. Bob has the rare gift of being able to think profoundly and play tennis at the same time. While laying me low with his forehand, he has regularly forced me to reassess my cherished beliefs. He has an unrivaled way of reducing complex questions and large swaths of history down to their elemental parts. When I wrote, and rewrote, this book, I was always thinking about whether Bob would find it illuminating and useful. I'm not at all sure that I've succeeded in this effort, but if this book has any lasting value, I owe it to him.

Last but not least, I need to thank Fouad Ajami, who now splits his time between the Hoover Institution and Johns Hopkins University. I first read *The Arab Predicament* soon after leaving Egypt. It was an intellectual feast: I found a means to make sense of what I'd seen, of what had saddened me. His book *The Vanished Imam* provides an unrivaled searchlight for scanning the Middle East. It is also a work of beauty and passion: I had it with me always when I was searching for Iranians who wanted to break bread with a CIA case officer. I would not have written *The Wave* if Fouad had not asked me to do so; I would have been lost in the Middle East years earlier without his guidance. Throughout the writing of this book, he was always there peppering me with questions and offering gentle advice. No *murshid* is responsible for the errors of a *murid*; Fouad cannot be blamed for what I have produced.

REUEL MARC GERECHT
October 2010

The Crisis of the Autocracies

H ow powerful is the idea of democracy in the Middle East? Could the region actually be at the beginning of a democratic wave, as potentially momentous as the nationalist upwelling after World War II? Could democratic convulsions even become the defining theme of the Middle East during Barack Obama's presidency? Freedom House, the chronicler of global democratic progress, tells us the opposite: a "democratic recession" is under way in Islamic lands. It remains gospel in much of the West that there really is an Arab-Islamic exception to representative government. Cultures always have unique compartmented quarters: that democracy triumphed in Japan and South Korea (with the Americans always nearby) does not necessarily mean that the Muslim Middle East can overcome its "oriental" difficulties (especially when the Americans are leaving). What Harvard's late Samuel Huntington flatly noted in 1991 is still true: "In practice, with one exception, no Islamic country has sustained a fully democratic political system for any length of time. The exception is Turkey, where Mustafa Kemal Atatürk explicitly rejected Islamic concepts of society and politics and vigorously attempted to create a secular, modern, Western nation-state. [And] Turkey's experience with democracy has not been an unmitigated success." But what if Professor Huntington's "third wave"—the extraordinary advance of democracy between 1974 and 1990—is arriving in the Middle East just a little late? Iranians and Arabs, *comme d'habitude*, always prefer to come late to a party.

All of this probably sounds surreal to many Americans and Europeans. A decade and two wars after 9/11, Western interest in and fear of the Middle East are waning. We have almost forgotten the spring of 2003, when the Washington foreign-policy establishment saw the expansion of democracy as critical to the solution of the Middle East's awful problems. Mainstream American liberals and conservatives then saw better, more representative, government as a crucial antidote to the social dysfunction and moral distemper that had produced Bin Ladenism, the deadly, Westerner-targeted Sunni Islamic militancy that started growing in the Muslim world as Osama bin Laden was becoming a holy-warrior celebrity in Saudi Arabia in the 1980s.

But Iraq, Afghanistan, a general feeling among many Middle Eastern observers that Bin Ladenism is now in retreat among Arabs, and the triumph of Hamas, the terrorism-loving Islamist party, in the US-backed Palestinian elections in 2005 have made democracy promotion among Muslims a difficult idea to swallow in the West. Liberal internationalism, which reflexively supported the expansion of democracy abroad for five decades and could at times even pressure Middle Eastern dictators to liberalize their societies (remember John F. Kennedy versus Mohammad Reza Pahlavi), now appears moribund within the Democratic Party. President Obama's outreach to Muslims, though still a work in progress, is so far exclusively cultural—an American variation of former Iranian President Mohammad Khatami's "dialogue of civilizations."

Read Mr. Obama's Islam-sensitive "New Beginning" Cairo oration in June 2009 next to Secretary of State Condoleezza Rice's June 2005 Cairo speech, and it's clear how little Washington is now concerned with the region's internal governance. Where Secretary Rice enumerated the human rights violations of countries by name and referred to the region's democratic dissidents as "impatient patriots . . . in Baghdad and Beirut, in Riyadh and Ramallah, in Amman and Tehran, and right here in Cairo," President Obama criticized no one by name, except for Israel and Hamas.

Democracy promotion is inextricably tied to George W. Bush's legacy. Any Democrat who adopts the cause also adopts, however distantly, former President Bush. It is worth recalling what Mr. Bush said in November 2003, nine months after the United States and Great Britain had invaded Iraq. He, more explicitly than any president before him, challenged the idea of "Islamic exceptionalism":

> In many nations of the Middle East—countries of great strategic importance—democracy has not yet taken root. And the questions arise: Are the peoples of the Middle East somehow beyond the reach of liberty? Are millions of men and women and children condemned by history or culture to live in despotism? Are they alone never to know freedom, and never even to have a choice in the matter? I, for one, do not believe it. I believe every person has the ability and the right to be free . . . Sixty years of Western nations excusing and accommodating the lack of freedom in the Middle East did nothing to make us safe—because in the long run, stability cannot be purchased at the expense of liberty. As long as the Middle East remains a place where freedom does not flourish, it will remain a place of stagnation, resentment, and violence ready for export. And with the spread of weapons that can bring catastrophic harm to our country and to our friends, it would be reckless to accept the status quo.

President Obama may have many reasons why he half-heartedly juxtaposes democracy, human rights, and Islam in his speeches, but remembering Mr. Bush is probably enough to ensure that he doesn't turn into a public booster of representative government among the Middle East's Muslims. The democratic convulsions within Iran may eventually change Mr. Obama's mind, and senior White House officials are quick to confess that the president regrets how tepidly he rose to praise the Green Movement and condemn Tehran's crackdown in the summer of 2009. Millions of Iranians hitting the streets to protest a fraudulent election and millions of Iraqis casting votes for the third time since the fall of Saddam Hussein have made many people—possibly even President Obama—reassess whether democracy just might have a future in the region.

They should reassess. Modern Middle Eastern autocracies may still be functioning police states, but they are being outflanked by forces that deny these regimes the requisite legitimacy for survival. There are two powerful—likely unstoppable—democratic movements in the Middle East. One is from the left and comprehensible to any Westerner who knows his past; the other, dubious and disorienting to Westerners, comes from the Islamic Right, which is much more comfortable talking about man's duties to God than about civil rights. The leftist movement has produced an avalanche of books, magazines, and articles over twenty-five years; the other has produced relatively few epistles and speeches. The leftists have developed under an increasingly brutal autocracy that nevertheless has allowed—could not stop—a constant exchange of ideas about God's and man's dominions. The rightists have developed in police states that have much more effectively shut down unauthorized reflection.

Iran's Green Movement is the real thing: a more or less liberal democratic movement, increasingly secular in philosophy and political objectives, rooted in Iran's large middle class and even larger pool of college-educated youth (a college education in Iran, where the revolution of 1979 zealously opened universities to the poor, doesn't denote membership in any economic class). The *jonbesh-e sabz*, as it is known in Persian, is increasingly similar in its aspirations and methods to what transpired behind the Iron Curtain before 1989. The disciples of the late Grand Ayatollah Hossein Ali Montazeri, whom Ayatollah Ruhollah Khomeini at first designated as his successor and then put under house arrest for questioning the propriety of the supreme leader's many executions, and other lesser-known traditional but reform-minded divines comprise this movement's conservative wing; but the secular brains of the Greens arose in the *tier-mondiste* whirlwind that downed the shah. It is the most recent manifestation—Mohammad Khatami's unexpected landslide presidential victory in 1997 was the first—of widespread female anger at the second-class citizenship accorded to women in the Islamic republic. Although the Green Movement is not well known in the West, its intellectual germination is the most momentous story in contemporary Iranian history. It is unique in the Middle East: an intellectual revolution that aims to solve peacefully and democratically the great Muslim torment about authenticity and cultural collaboration. How do a proud people adopt the best (and the worst) from the West and remain true to their much-loved historical identity? The Green Movement provokes the question of whether Iran will be a trailblazer for others. Can similar Arab democratic movements develop without religious revolutions pushing intellectuals first through the soul-crushing unpleasantness of a theocratic state?

Powerful liberal democratic movements may not have developed throughout the Arab world, but Islamist-driven movements have. For many in the West and the Middle East, the idea of an Islamist-driven democratic movement seems oxymoronic and frightening. It is certainly an unsettled question whether devout Muslims—especially Arab Muslims who are intimately bound by language to the Qur'an and the prophetic traditions—can generate a system where free elections determine who governs. What Alexis de Tocqueville wrote in the 1830s still stands as the greatest challenge for any Muslim who believes in the immutability of the Shariah, the Holy Law:

> Mohammad professed to derive from Heaven, and has inserted in the Koran, not only religious doctrines, but political maxims, civil and criminal laws, and theories of science. The Gospel, on the contrary, speaks only of the general relations of men to God and to each other, beyond which it inculcates and imposes no point of faith. This alone, besides a thousand other reasons, would suffice to prove that the former of these religions will never long predominate in a cultivated and democratic age, while the latter is destined to retain its sway at these . . . periods.

But the fundamentalist embrace of democratic politics as a vehicle for removing secular dictatorships in the Arab world is now the rule, not the exception. Where once Islamist groups dreamed of revolution, quietly developed paramilitary cells, and assassinated their secular opponents, mainstream Islamist groups today, most of which are descended from Egypt's Muslim Brotherhood, see elections as a means for society to maintain its *akhlaq*, the mores that define good Muslims. Although it is at times difficult to gauge the likely popularity of the devout at the urns, it is a decent bet that in every Arab land—but especially in Egypt—religious parties would do well, perhaps decisively so, in any free vote. In Algeria, the lodestar of the Arab West, where the collision of election-winning fundamentalists and the military junta in 1992 produced civil war, and where many Islamists, like the government's *exterminateur* security forces, resorted to terrifying violence, slaughtering innocents because they were innocent, a reborn less-vengeful Islamic Salvation Front might still gain a plurality in a free vote.

Nowhere have Arab secular dictatorships produced liberalizing, less religious societies. Algeria in 2010 appears just as religious as it was in 1990. It may well be more religious, as the horrific bloodletting has left the entire country in a mournful daze, where faith can at least provide some solace. Algeria's non-religious intelligentsia, which split over the military's nullification of parliamentary elections in 1991, still cannot bring itself to embrace the government, which no longer even tries to inspire the citizenry.

Arab dictators—especially Egypt's Hosni Mubarak—have made an art of scaring and convincing American administrations that their autocracies are the only thing that stands in the way of a fundamentalist tidal wave. The Bush administration—even its most ardent proponents of democracy abroad—never really wanted to test their claims, hoping against evidence that these governments would slowly loosen their grip and allow for liberal secular Muslims to gain strength (à la the Turkish example of Mustafa Kemal Atatürk and his successor Ismet Inönü). But no secular Arab dictatorship has yet shown that it can compete with religious organizations for hearts and votes. In most Arab lands, fundamentalism appears to be gaining ground among the urban middle and even upper classes—the civilian bedrock of Arab secular dictatorship and the historic breeding ground of liberal, secular Arabs. The expansion of the urban middle class—an occasional aspiration of the regimes in Egypt, Algeria, Tunisia, Jordan, and Syria—now probably guarantees greater sympathy for the faithful than for secular liberals.

Egypt deserves our special consideration, given its trailblazing role among Arab states, which still hasn't ended even with its enormous problems. Egypt's population alone—around 80 million—makes it the Arab world's only heavyweight. Muslim fundamentalists are politically stronger there than anywhere else west of Iran; so, too, somewhat less obviously, are liberals. Any movement away from dictatorship could easily have regional repercussions. Over the years, a legion of academics and pundits has predicted the collapse of the Mubarak government only to see the regime sputter on. The Nile River Valley, where civilization exists in a narrow band, is an authoritarian's dream landscape. Egyptian liberals, as well as fundamentalists, have been hit hard by Mubarak. Indeed, the saga of Ayman Nour, a forty-one-year-old lawyer, who rose in 2005 to challenge Mubarak in the presidential election, is the depressing story, writ large, of liberalism in the Arab Middle East.

Nour was an unlikely opponent of dictatorship. He was no firebrand; he was quiet and soft-spoken. He was a sitting parliamentarian, formerly a member of Egypt's historic nationalist Wafd Party, which he left in 2000 because of its lack of commitment to liberal reform. In October 2004, he registered his own party, the *Ghad*, which means "tomorrow" in Arabic. Nour was realistic. He knew that his chances of winning against Mubarak were impossibly remote. But his mission was to get his word out in the 18 days of allowed campaigning. For Nour the election was a small and limited step on the road to representative government. He posed no great threat to Mubarak and his National Democratic Party. Yet this young lawyer was, nonetheless, perhaps considered a possible adversary for Mubarak's son Gamal, who has made it clear that he wants to succeed his father and fancies himself a "progressive." Dissident liberals (a different species than "court liberals," who applaud their ruler's generosity and Westernized wisdom) inevitably get bludgeoned in the Middle East by more "liberal" authoritarians. American and European diplomats and optimistic newspaper columnists often see these rulers as having promise since Westerners can see liberal cultural sentiments within these possibly "transformational" figures. Whether Muslim liberal dissidents have any real vote-getting power is irrelevant (and in Egypt, liberals could well garner serious minority power given the country's long and intimate absorption of Western culture); Westernized dictators strike liberal dissidents since they are challenging secular autocracy on social and cultural terrain that properly belongs to the ruling elite. Liberal dissidents, unlike the more numerous and powerful fundamentalists, can elicit the support of the West, which can be especially annoying to Westernized autocrats constantly seeking trade, aid, and weaponry from America and Europe.

And so the inevitable happened. In January 2005, Nour was arrested for allegedly forging signatures to register his party for the upcoming election. Soon, though, international reaction proved too strong. Secretary of State Rice canceled a visit. Under American and European pressure, the regime released Nour, who campaigned and received 8 percent of the vote to Mubarak's 89 percent. In the days immediately preceding the elections, Nour spoke to the BBC. When questioned about his concern over being arrested again and perhaps convicted, the liberal dissident replied that he believed in justice and Egypt's judges. His trust was misplaced, and he was rearrested just days after the elections. In December 2005, Nour was found guilty and sentenced to five years in prison. The judge—a known Mubarak supporter—was the same judge who sentenced the pro-democracy activist Saad Eddin Ibrahim to prison in 2002. While in prison, Nour wrote to then-presidential candidate Barack Obama and appealed to him "to help Arab reformers push for democracy in the Middle East." In February 2009, after three years in prison, Nour was released, quite possibly as a small olive branch to the new administration in Washington.

In September 2011, Egypt is scheduled to have its next presidential election. As of this writing in the summer of 2010, the country was holding its breath, as *The Economist* put it in a special survey of Egypt in July 2010. With Mubarak reportedly in ill health, the question arose as to whether the president would grant himself another six-year term or engineer the succession to power of his son. Mubarak faced two foes—his longtime nemesis, the Muslim Brotherhood, and a new antagonist, Mohamed ElBaradei, the former director general of the International Atomic Energy Agency. But there were questions as to whether ElBaradei was fully committed to contest the elections in 2011. ElBaradei divided his time between Cairo and his home in France, and though his fans on Facebook were said to number a quarter-million with more joining each day, he seemed to be merely flirting with the political process. His "national association for change" sought to create a more competitive political environment where elections would be meaningful. But it was unclear whether an expatriate, nurtured in international organizations, had the wherewithal and will to shake Egypt's dictatorial institutions. Still, ElBaradei was something new in Egypt—an uncorrupted outsider whose international stature guaranteed him an independent voice. He became the center of attention in great part because he had tapped into a widespread sentiment that something big needed to change in the country. Whether or not ElBaradei considered himself a serious contender for the presidency, his legions of followers and their campaign to defeat Mubarak led to a redoubling of efforts by Mubarak and the NDP to maintain and tighten their grip on power. Protesters and activists were facing down the government during the summer of 2010, demanding greater political freedom, electoral reform, higher wages, and better working conditions. Was this the "summer of Egyptian discontent," or will all this blow over with the regime holding firm to power? Like Egypt's first truly modern dictator, Gamal Abdel Nasser, Hosni Mubarak has built the most sophisticated police state in the Middle East, utilizing a massive, Stasi-like array of informants, pervasive wiretapping, and in Cairo an extensive and modern means of video surveillance on the streets. (Anwar Sadat, Nasser's successor, was no democrat; but there was chaos and haphazardness in the way he ruled and he was sensitive to the judgment of Western democracies.) If the Egyptian security apparatus holds firm, political evolution won't happen. In uncertain autocracies, loyalties are fluid. If Mubarak is alive and not running, he will likely rig the election—though by how much and for whom remain unclear. The regime may well coalesce around Gamal to avoid political turmoil. But even among Mubarak's die-hard supporters, there is palpable unease about his son succeeding him. Hypocrisy defines Egypt's political class, which is why the government jails and tortures those who publicly mock the Mubarak family. (There probably isn't a member of the ruling elite who doesn't mock them privately.) Corruption is a sensitive issue. Dynastic succession remains distasteful in republican Egypt. Egyptians remember, even if Westerners do not, that riots have occasionally shaken the police state. (The bread riots of 1977 traumatized the country and reminded everyone that the have-nots really do resent the haves.) Even Egypt's controlled press occasionally alludes to the ticking time bombs that develop when wealthy people flaunt their "success" in a desperately poor country.

Egypt has become a land of stark extremes: in Cairo multi-million dollar riverine apartments and lushly watered exurban golf courses built on sand look out upon an endless horizon of low-rising, nearly windowless, brick apartment buildings, which are virtually uninhabitable during Egypt's summer. These "homes" are stuffed with urban peasants— the mythical, now deracinated *fellaheen*—who *can* see progress (Cairo is a vibrant mess of a modern city). Egypt's acid-tongued poor can read. Sixty years of socialist-turned-capitalist dictatorship have certainly given the Egyptian masses sufficient education to dream; it's given the bright among the poor and the country's growing middle class the means to aspire. Like much of the Middle East without oil, Egypt is growing economically. Using the standard set by Samuel Huntington, Egypt economically isn't that far from the democratic "transition zone," where a society's complexities start to overload centralized authoritarian states and where dreams actually become tangible.

The year 2011 might, just possibly, be decisive. If the intellectual and popular forces that almost spontaneously created the Green Movement can hold on against the supreme leader Ali Khameneh'i (and the odds are decent that they can), and Egypt comes into play, the reluctant and embarrassed Western conversation about democracy among Muslims will seem as astute as those voices who argued that Islamic radicalism and terrorism were actually declining threats in the 1990s. It is very good to recall that the West and the Iranian state were blindsided by the rise of Khatami in 1997 and the Green Movement in 2009. Each movement was crushed by the regime—the Green Movement requiring much more brutality to suppress than did the youth rebellion behind Khatami a decade earlier. Authoritarianism in Egypt has been more effective in shutting down debate, but the Egyptian opposition, especially the Muslim Brotherhood, which can attract followers and organize even in a police state, continues to flourish. It is only a matter of time—and probably far less time than conventional "realist" wisdom would lead us to believe—before democratic conversations in the Middle East drown out all the other discussions, perhaps even the constant background noise of the Israeli-Palestinian confrontation.

We may well know by 2012 whether Khameneh'i's regime is going to get a nuclear weapon, which will leave the Greens as the only possible internal means to halt (or reverse) its deployment. By 2012 we will likely know whether the Israelis have tried to derail Tehran's nuclear program through preventive military strikes, which will also underscore the fact that as long as Iran remains Khameneh'i's Islamic republic, a virulently anti-Semitic, increasingly paranoid Islamist nuclear state is in our future.

By 2012 we should have a better idea whether Iraq's democratic *modus vivendi*, no longer guaranteed by the US military, will be enough for the Arab Shiites, the Kurds and the Sunni Arabs, whose revanchist dreams launched the insurgency and still allow radical Sunni groups a foothold in the country. If Iraqi democracy keeps staggering forward, its politics will inevitably become a factor elsewhere. Even a casual observer of the Middle East's Arabic-language satellite channels can see that the Sunni Arab world doesn't quite know how to handle an Iraq where Sunni Iraqis vote and applaud the American presence in the country (as a counterweight to Shiite power). Shiite and Sunni Iraqi commentators who express no remorse about the fall of Saddam Hussein and discuss their political battles in Baghdad—especially when they asperse each other and call into question the wisdom of their elected leadership—regularly leave other Arab guests in the astonishing position of being dictatorial toadies jousting with Arabs who meaningfully vote or serve in a parliament that actually has power. The Sunni Arab canon not to say anything good about Iraq is fraying, more actually than it has in the anti-war mainstream of the Democratic Party. The effect of this on the region may not be small in the coming years.

Sooner not later, we need to understand how deeply democratic ideas have penetrated the Middle East. We need to appreciate the fragility of Iran's dictatorship, and how Iranians could do what liberal Arab Muslims failed to do in the 1920s and 1930s: create a viable liberal democracy. Ali Khameneh'i's crackdown on the Green Movement has been brutal and effective. The regime's security apparatus may well be successful for years to come in squelching the opposition. But intellectually the world has nearly turned upside down. In the ways that Khameneh'i probably thinks matter most, the supreme leader now rules over a foreign country. Philosophically and spiritually, Iranians are actually exiting the Islamic revolution more like Westerners than when Mohammad Reza Pahlavi imagined his countrymen to be the Germans of the Middle East.

We also need—perhaps above all else—to understand better the most troubling Muslim-Western hybrid: the Arab fundamentalists who believe they can save their societies through God and democracy. Their past—their long and complicated evolution—makes them the strongest democratic standard-bearers from Jordan to Morocco. They, not the Ayman Nours, who naturally appeal to Westerners, have real street power. They are undoubtedly alarming, yet they also offer probably the best hope—however counterintuitive it seems—for Arab societies to escape the political sclerosis and spiritual rot that led to Osama bin Laden becoming a popular hero.

More so than the Persians and the Turks, who with the Arabs are the three peoples who have driven Islamic history, the children of Hagar have the heaviest baggage to carry into modernity. Democracy has been so often aborted in Arab countries that many Western observers understandably are skeptical that Arabs will ever escape their "oriental despotisms." Arab democratic dissidents often appear second-rate and far less numerous when compared to their Iranian counterparts, who are more comprehensive and trenchant in their critiques of authoritarianism and the faith. And Arab liberal dissidents regularly seem deeply conflicted about priorities. Should anti-Zionism and Arab solidarity be downplayed or underscored in the quest for democracy at home?

Westerners are unlikely to understand the long complicated evolution of Arab fundamentalists—and how they are key to democracy's eventual success in the Middle East—unless they grasp how daunting are the Arabs' modern problems. Owing to history, faith, and language, the Arabs have found it maddeningly difficult to import the West's most successful political experiment. Americans, in particular, poorly appreciate the force of language on history (an American statesman would never write a book titled *A History of the English-Speaking Peoples*). Yet its influence has been centripetal: the Qur'an, the Prophet Muhammad, the great and glorious classical period of Islamic history are always looming in speech, poetry, and literature, shaping the way even die-hard atheists see themselves. It's probably not a coincidence that Turkey has made more democratic progress than any other land in the Middle East and that Turkish, since Atatürk's linguistic reforms, is alphabetically, and even spiritually, distant from Arabic. The added distance, which has been infused with Turkish national pride and (largely invented) pre-Islamic Turkic history, gives maneuvering room to those who want to import foreign ideas into the national consciousness. Where once Ottoman gentlemen would command three languages (Arabic for religion, Persian for beauty, and Turkish for war), today's Turkish elite, even among the most religious, are much more likely to know a Western language.

And Arab-Muslim pride married to anti-imperialism produced an acute intellectual openness to the dark side of Western history. The empowering collective appeal of socialism and fascism was pervasive before and after World War II. Although the use of the word *hurriya*, "freedom" in Arabic, has increasingly drawn closer to its Western sense of individual liberty, it still resonates with the idea of "national liberation." Unlike in India where British-imported democratic practices and ideals became a powerful vehicle driving independence, the spirit of representative government quickly evanesced among Arab elites, who much more enthusiastically lauded national strength and ethnic pride without much reference to voting rights. Throughout much of the region, civilians lost control to officers, who were by far the best-organized and the most Westernized professionals. The militarization of the Muslim Arab world's most urban and advanced societies—Egypt, Iraq, Algeria, and Syria—ensued. And oil wealth—even in countries like Egypt that have little—snaked its way through the region, feeding armies and intelligence services before it fed the people. The distance between rulers and ruled has been great in the Islamic world since broad-based tribal structures gave way to slave soldiers in the ninth century. Talented military slaves became the elite; freemen became serfs. Oil has cursed the Arabs (and the Iranians) again with authoritarian regimes that need little from those they rule. Many Arab autocrats—not just Saddam Hussein, who rivaled Stalin and Mao in his barbarism—have made Mohammad Reza Pahlavi, Iran's last shah, look like a relatively liberal, Swiss-educated *bon vivant*.

Arab intellectuals, as the Johns Hopkins and Hoover Institution historian Fouad Ajami has written, have been caught in a "dream palace," where there is an extraordinary rupture between aspirations and reality. It is astonishing how few Arab intellectuals—especially in the large and talented diaspora—have engaged in damning critiques of their homelands and *the* philosophical handmaiden of tyranny: pan-Arabism. Given the enormous economic problems throughout the region, given the aesthetic wreckage of its landscape, architecture, and cultural institutions, given how socialist and state-capitalist autocrats have caused more suffering to Arabs than communists did to Eastern Europeans, and given how loquacious Arabs are, one might have expected tidal waves of damning critiques of contemporary Arab history—of the passions that moved Arabs in such self-destructive ways since the Europeans departed. And even when well-known liberal Arab intellectuals have strongly criticized the kings and presidents-for-life, and the late Palestinian-American Edward Said is an excellent example, the accompanying criticisms of the West usually drown out the admonishments of the natives. (And in Said's case, the attacks on Arab tyranny always seem to revolve around the Palestinians and the failure of Arabs against Zionists.) The Lebanese-American Fouad Ajami, the Iraqi-American intellectual Kanan Makiya, the Palestinian journalist Sa'id K. Abu-Rish, and the former Iraqi minister Ali Allawi are such surprises when one first reads them because they focus more on what Arabs do to themselves and less on what foreigners have done to Arabs. As a class, Arab intellectuals have done considerable damage to the democratic and liberal aspirations of their countrymen. The philosophical scaffolding for Arab democracy—especially liberal democracy—is so weak in part because so few great minds have given it much thought.

And last but not least among the Arab world's debilitating problems, the region has been the primary beneficiary of Saudi missionary activity. Little has been written about how Saudi Arabia's great wealth has aided the "Wahhabization" of the Middle East. Wahhabism, the eighteenth-century offshoot of the Hanbali rite, the youngest and most rigorous of Sunni Islam's law schools, offers the most severe—the Ottomans thought it un-Islamic—interpretation of the Shariah. Saudi money and Wahhabi thought have remade the religious map of the Sunni world since 1979, when Saudi Arabia, threatened by Iran's monarchy-loathing Shiite revolution, counterattacked with unprecedented levels of proselytizing. Sunni Islam's other schools—especially the more tolerant traditions of the Hanafi rite, the dominant practice within the Ottoman Empire—and Sufism, the great peaceful vehicle of Islamic expansion in Central and Eastern Asia, have taken a beating. Qur'anic literalists, Wahhabis are virulently hostile to the idea of parliaments legislating laws and morality. (When the Saudi court formally abolished slavery in 1962, Wahhabi clerics, who undergird the Saudi state, did not rise in jubilation.) Saudi largesse has helped to change the center of gravity in the Middle East, making fundamentalism a mainstream belief.

It is impossible now to imagine fundamentalists being, as the secular Egyptian democratic dissident Saad Eddin Ibrahim put it, "cavalierly excluded" from the democratic process. What the Saudis have in part wrought is now inextricably part of the fabric of the region. If democracy is to succeed in Arab lands, it will be because devout Arabs have decided that their faith and representative government can meld. Indeed, if liberalism ever triumphs among Muslim Arabs, it will likely be courtesy of liberal-unfriendly fundamentalists who opened the political systems.

And to the north of Arabs and Iranians, we also must look at the Turks, for centuries the most powerful of Islam's three most formative peoples. Alone among the Middle East's Muslims, Turks have exited decades of secular, pro-Western authoritarianism into democracy. As should have been expected, though by many was not, more representative government in Turkey has re-injected more Islam into politics as the secularized Istanbul and Ankara elites have had to give ground to the rising economic and political power of the Anatolian faithful. The amplification of the Muslim component in the Turkish identity has had several unpleasant side effects: more anti-Americanism, anti-Zionism, and anti-Semitism. This is the unholy trinity of democratic expansion among Muslims who've lived under right-wing secular authoritarianism, especially if the governments in question had close ties with the United States and Israel. (Movement in the opposite direction is occurring in Iran, where Iranian intellectuals have moved away from the themes of the Islamic republic's foundation.)

Turkey's rising Muslim identity has accentuated the debate about whether democracy can survive in a Muslim land if it's not built on a resolutely, perhaps even authoritarian, secular foundation. The old Turkish elite, like the pro-Turkish sentiments once common in both Washington and Jerusalem, arose from Kemalist policies that heavily circumscribed religious expression. Turkey's ruling Islamist-sympathetic *Adalet ve Kalkinma Partisi*, "The Justice and Development Party," better known under its initials, AKP, has worked arduously to ensure that the undemocratic but constitutional means used to check the political power of Islamist political parties in the past are neutralized. Relishing its political strength, which is based on a 30–40 percent slice of the electorate, the AKP has sought by legal, sometimes legally dubious, and often abusive means to undermine those in the army, the judiciary, and the Istanbul business community—the pillars of the Kemalist state—that have opposed it.

As a result, much to the dismay of old-time Kemalists, Turkey has become a laboratory for Islamists and democracy. If the Turks, who've been Westernized far more profoundly than other Muslims in the Middle East and who've built a vibrant economy on trade and industry, cannot sustain the transition to democracy, then it certainly casts doubts on whether the Arabs ever can. Islamic revanchism against secular autocracy could play out democratically in Turkey: eventually the AKP will lose an election and the secular crowd will regain power. It could possibly end in another military coup, which would, for the very first time, probably pit the army against a sizable portion of the population. Or it could effectively transform Turkey into a one-party state. Since Abdülmecid II, the last occupant of the Dolmabaçe Palace, was exiled to Switzerland in 1924, the country has never been in more play. The Turkish identity, once again, is in flux. Turks don't know where the return of history is taking them.

And last but not least we need to look at Americans, who are more confused now than ever before about what to do in the Middle East. President Obama has promised a new "dialogue of civilizations" with the Muslim world. Mohammad Khatami's dialogue with the West never got off the ground because the Iranian president was unwilling to cross swords with Ali Khameneh'i. Yet comparing Khatami with Obama gives a means of better assessing what America should do in the Middle East. Obama, who mentions Islam, the birth faith of his father, only elliptically in his autobiography, seems unaware that Islamic fundamentalism has become part of the Muslim mainstream. In Cairo, the president spoke about "the harmony between tradition and progress" by juxtaposing Egypt's and Sunni Islam's oldest center of learning, Al-Azhar, with Cairo University, once one of the region's finest modern schools. But these two institutions, and what they represent, have been in a tug-of-war, always philosophical, sometimes violent, for over a hundred years. It was this lack of harmony—the constant tension between the Muslim search for authenticity and the Muslim love of Westernization—that brought down Mohammad Khatami.

Although a democratic culture hasn't yet prevailed anywhere in the Middle East outside of Turkey (in Iran, it's getting close), millions of Iranians and Arabs clearly want to have a go at it. *Masuliyat*—"responsibility"—is a seldom-used word in the conspiracy-obsessed Middle East, even by the region's political elites. But that is changing, from the bottom up in Arab lands, and in Iran, even more powerfully, from the top down. When Iranians and Arabs have been given a chance to vote, even in controlled elections, they've shown eagerness and vexing independence (as have the Turks, who've increasingly strayed from the politics and the parties that ran the Kemalist state). Anyone who has spent time with Iranians and Egyptians knows how wide the gulf is between their glorious self-image and their impoverished reality. In both countries, democracy is now widely seen as the only answer to national decline. In both countries, as in Iraq, there are good (if inaccurately recalled) memories of an earlier, better democratic age.

Although violence has defined the political culture of the modern Middle East, Iran and Egypt—among the first modernizing Muslim states—have a chance of making a democratic transition without the internecine strife that we saw in Iraq, Algeria, the West Bank, and Gaza. Ask an Egyptian or an Iranian whether democracy means chaos—a favorite theme of President Mubarak and Iran's most eloquent defender of theocracy Ayatollah Mohammad Taqi Mesbah-Yazdi—and you are unlikely to hear a sympathetic response. President George W. Bush might have been an evangelical democracy-loving character out of Alexis de Tocqueville's *De la Démocratie en Amérique*, but the Texan perhaps captured a truth that more worldly men missed. The idea of democracy, once it secretes itself into the body politic, is durable and aggressive. Philosophically, it inevitably puts divine and mundane autocrats on defense. (Francis Fukuyama definitely got this right.) It becomes ever more authentic, much to the dismay of Westernized dictators, tribal kings, and Occidentals skeptical about the propriety of their exports.

The Iranians

PERHAPS THE MOST IMPORTANT FACT to remember about
the Islamic revolution is how popular it was among well-
educated Iranians. Of all the Iranian teachers and students
I've known, of all the Iranian exiles I've met on four
continents over three decades, very few of them were actually
for the shah in 1978. Most were passionately for Ayatollah
Khomeini. It took them a while to realize what the great
Marxist (one-time Stalinist) French orientalist Maxime
Rodinson saw quickly: Khomeini was really Tomás de
Torquemada. The Iranian educated class, long alienated from
the Pahlavi dynasty, abandoned the *ancien régime*. There are
many reasons why secular Arab dictatorships did not succumb
to Islamic revolutions after 1979 even though Iran's rebellion
was enormously appealing to devout and angry Arab Muslims.
Having the benefit of seeing Iran's revolution quickly devolve
into bloody internecine strife, where the radicalized urban
poor ate middle-class revolutionaries, Arab elites hung on
tightly to their corrupt Westernized autocrats. They have
hung on to them ever since, although their grip is loosening.

Thirty years on, it is still difficult to isolate all the intellectual components that went into the left-wing-Shiite Islamist Molotov cocktail that exploded into revolution. Although

the Middle East was awash with Marxism after World War II, the Iranian fascination with class-based analysis and anger was acute. The Iranian communist party, the *Tudeh*, which means "the masses" in Persian, was the strongest communist party in the Middle East. It had a near vise grip on the best and brightest who'd been produced at home and abroad by Reza Shah's and his son's determination to have a Westernized, well-educated elite.

Historically, Shiism has developed as a creed for the oppressed (Sunnis being the oppressors). The marriage of Marxism and Shiism was natural, even for those who believed in God more than Marx. Ayatollah Morteza Mottahari, a founding father of the Islamic revolution and close associate of Khomeini's who made a specialty of critiquing Marxists who draped themselves in the faith, published important works explaining Shiism and its revolutionary mission. His *Resurrection* could just as well have been used by Latin-American socialist revolutionaries to enlist Jesus in their cause. Separating Marx from God among Iran's "red mullahs" was a task that even the most intellectually sensitive clerics could not do. And if divines couldn't do it, lay intellectuals were hopeless.

Iran's democratic evolution is unique and profound in the Middle East precisely because the Iranian elite's commitment to left-wing causes was so thorough. Iranians combined God with Marx fervently. As Iran's theocracy has spiritually imploded since the death of Khomeini in 1989 (Khameneh'i, Khomeini's charisma-free successor, was never going to carry the revolution's chiliastic expectations), this intricate weaving of God and man has nearly come apart. Soul-scorching self-criticism has followed in its place. Iranians have come so far so fast—a second "intellectual revolution," to borrow from the scholar Mehran Kamrava, has occurred in the country since 1989—because many of them have realized, especially among the pro-revolution intellectual elite, that they erred profoundly in their naive enthusiasm for the revolution. The enormous pride Iranians had in the revolution—they alone among the Muslim Middle East's oppressed peoples actually pulled one off—has converted into reflection and self-criticism. The real Iranian revolutionaries, the ones who still believe in an Iranian *mission civilisatrice*, are the big men of the Green Movement—Mir Hussein Moussavi, Mehdi Karroubi, and even the weaker-willed Mohammad Khatami—and, as importantly, the lesser-known intellectual heavyweights who have literally rebuilt Iran mentally and morally since 1989.

Conspiracy theories still punctuate Iranian conversations. Conspiracies are spiritual safety valves in societies where power always operates *posht-e pardeh*, "behind the curtain." It is a crutch for people who want to avoid responsibility for their own actions. But *towtieh-ju'i*, "conspiracy-mongering," is much less vibrant in the ruminations of Iran's pro-democracy writers of the past twenty-five years. The Islamic republic is no longer chiefly the victim of titanic forces—the Americans, Russians, or British. These intellectuals do not recast history—rare is the Iranian writer like Abbas Milani, a historian at Stanford University, who can honestly look at the 1953 coup against Prime Minister Mohammad Mosaddeq and say that Iranians, especially senior members of the clergy, were as instrumental to that coup's success as were American or British intelligence officers. Few Iranian intellectuals care to remember, as Milani does, that Mosaddeq was no angel and that the *Tudeh* really was a serious challenge to both monarch and parliament. The West's real and imagined sins still often figure prominently in the thoughts of Iran's reformist intellectuals. But there is perspective now where earlier there was none.

In 1979 Iranians became responsible for their own fate. Exiled monarchists may love to blame the revolution on Jimmy Carter, the CIA, and the British foreign intelligence service MI6. But the men who actually made the revolution, and their sons and daughters, certainly don't. Mohammad Khatami's famous books, *Fear of the Wave* and *From the World City to the City World*, are in great part about Iranians becoming intellectual adults. Behind Khatami's endless fascination with Western philosophy is the not-so-subtle theme that Iranians, and other third-world Muslims, can and must confront the intellectual and material awesomeness of the West. Iranians must remain true to themselves—to the nation, the faith, and the revolution. But they can and should evolve. Stasis—reflexive fear of the West—can only grievously wound both Iran and Islam. Self-confident adaptation is the key to an Islamic renaissance. The twenty million Iranians who voted for Khatami in 1997 (the evening before the election the ivory-towered affable cleric thought he'd get at best two million votes) were clearly saying that adaptation—that is, cultural collaboration with the West—wasn't a stumbling block.

Contemporary Iranian reflection on Ali Shariati (1933–1977)—the Marxist-Islamist father of the revolution—serves well to illustrate the enormous change in Iran. Even more than Khomeini's writings on the clergy and an Islamic state, Shariati's works were instrumental in developing the religious national pride and righteous indignation that was the jet fuel for Khomeini's later assault on the shah in the 1970s. Shariati blended Shiism's rich history of heroic martyrs, a Nietzschean love of supermen, third-world-friendly Marxism (Frantz

Fanon), a touch of Sigmund Freud, a dash of Jean-Paul Sartre and Martin Heidegger, and a big splash of the nineteenth-century, anticolonial, globe-trotting, free-spirited über-Muslim nationalist, Jamal ad-Din al-Afghani.

A Westerner (at least this one) can have a hard time reading Shariati's speeches that he gave in Tehran in the 1960s and 1970s as works of history, philosophy, or political reflection. They are a mind-bending mess of ideas that are, at times, almost impossible to follow. But they do emote. Shariati had a genius for university-educated Iranians' central nervous system. He knew their guilt and shame (simultaneously loving and loathing the West and their own culture). He could project their deepest desire to triumph simultaneously over their own weaknesses and the West. Perhaps above all else, he could sense the faith dying for his own kind—Iranians who'd imbibed enough of the West to neuter a conception of the divine that gives bliss, solace, or sense of earthly and ethereal brotherhood. In its place, Shariati substituted action—power—as a creed. As with the socialist liberation theologians of Latin America, faith for him could never happen while standing still. One's soul became the public square. Islam's profound preference for orthopraxy over orthodoxy—it's not what you believe (that's between you and God) but what you do outwardly as a Muslim that matters—made his politicization of the faith easier. Shiism was rolled into nationalism, nationalism into Shiism, and the whole thing lit on fire (not too difficult to do since the Iranian identity has been for a millennium overwhelmingly Islamic and for four hundred years inseparable from Shiism). Mixing Marx with Arab tribesmen, Shariati saw "Red Shiism" as the birth faith of Islam—the revolutionary quest of the prophet, his cousin and son-in-law Ali, his sons, and their descendants, to fight for justice, which means the liberation of the oppressed. But owing to the strength of the enemies arrayed against them, and as important, the weakness of Shiites themselves, "Black Shiism," the faith of autocrats and their submissive, always-mourning flock, stole Islamic history. Shariati was determined to take it back. Shiite quietism, the age-old recognition that fate was usually cruel to the followers of Ali, was replaced with a very modern, fearless quest for self-actualization.

In the 1960s and 1970s, Iranians were a potpourri of emotions as the old world died and the new world had not yet taken hold. Opportunities for middle-class Iranians and the poor were growing. A profoundly traditional people who'd become increasingly deracinated from their small-town roots and faith, Iranians were anxious. Shariati was that rare public intellectual: he could animate the past. In a way no cleric could, he made the Caliph Ali come alive. The historic Ali, like the Prophet Muhammad, is nearly impossible to see accurately in contemporary primary sources (the prophetic and early—"rightly-guided"—caliphal period isn't chronicled by Muslims until the eighth and ninth centuries, by which time certain images and story lines had undoubtedly become canonical). Shariati took the believers' historic affection and made the man into a modern-day progressive superhero. Where the historic Ali and his followers were likely animated by the all-consuming fear that without righteous leadership, Muslims individually would be unable to enter heaven, Shariati's Ali is a hero of the common man whose communal objectives are much more mundane than avoiding eternal damnation.

Shariati created a parallel religious world through the Hosseiniyeh Ershad Institute in Tehran—a place of religious education free of clerics (revolutionary leftists always have a hard time with clerics) where men of little real faith, like the French-educated, Sartre-admiring Shariati, could be proud believers and patriots. Shariati gave an imaginary religious history to left-wing Muslims that allowed them to remain Muslims—something they desperately wanted. Today in Lebanon, Iraq, Iran, and in the Shiite ghettos of Bahrain, a visitor can see flags of Ali and his son Hussein, Shiism's iconic martyr. It was Shariati—as much as Khomeini, or Lebanon's Hezbollah guide Mohammed Hussein Fadlallah, or Iraq's intellectually refined and charismatic Muhammad Baqir as-Sadr—who remade history so that Islam's creed of earthly suffering, quiet martyrdom, and resurrection, became a warrior's faith with flags and Qu'ranic-emblazoned headbands. One of my Persian-language tutors at the CIA, a soft-spoken man of even softer leftist convictions, nearly took my head off in 1986 when I suggested that Shariati might be the most overrated modern Iranian intellectual. His writings, so I thought, had aged poorly under Khomeini, who'd created a theocracy that Shariati surely would have reviled. For the "thinking Iranian," those who'd rather read poetry or a good novel than take another dip in the Qu'ran (probably the vast majority of Iranians, even perhaps in the holy city of Qom), Shariati was as sacred as Khomeini. My Persian tutor never forgave me for my misstep.

Yet Shariati's views are no longer holy. Indeed, the great intellectual ferment that defines Iranian society since the death of Khomeini in 1989—a ferment that has much greater literary depth (far more people read more books, newspapers, and magazines) than was the case in the 1960s and 1970s, when Iran's pro-revolutionary writers at home and abroad were far fewer and their production far less—has largely discarded Shariati's views. Where Shariati and his great intellectual brother, Jalal Al-e Ahmad, who introduced the word *gharbzadegi*, "Westoxification," into the Persian vocabulary, consumed left-wing Western philosophy to produce a virulently anti-Western creed, Iran's post-Khomeini intellectuals and dissident clerics have consumed, far more critically, a much larger range of Western thought and produced a view of the world that if not pro-Western is no longer anti-Western. These intellectuals and clerics are at ease discussing the West's achievements and sins, and often more concerned with dissecting Iran's "pathology of despotism" (Khatami) and the building blocks of the flawed Iranian character.

Although few Iranian intellectuals are as unsentimental in their reflections as Mahmood Sariolghalam, who teaches at Shahid Beheshti University, Iran's post-Khomeini intellectuals are in broad agreement with him about where the real devil lies. For Sariolghalam, whose intellectual elegance and wit have made him a widely read and much-admired thinker, the principal faults lie not in the West—in the lingering echoes of European imperialism, America's support of the shah, or the value-free consumerism that accompanies globalization. The biggest problems are overwhelmingly Iranian in origin, and the only solution is for Iranians to become much more rational in their personalities and democratic in their politics. "We need a new Iranian," Sariolghalam told us in 2003, "an Iranian who is responsible, fair, hardworking, devout but not fanatical, self-assured, self-motivated, knows limits, takes pride in his land, is willing to take criticism, is not gullible, and is not boastful." In person Sariolghalam can be arresting, a social scientist's curiosity married to an Iranian poet's concern for deep-rooted beauty. Always good-natured but unrepentant, he has kept his head down since the June 12, 2009 elections, but continues to teach.

But as the post–June 12 tumult revealed, the Iranian character has probably advanced further than what Sariolghalam thought possible when he was witnessing the collapse of Khatami's presidency. Iran's secular and religious dissidents went into a great funk when Khatami failed to stand his ground after Khameneh'i unleashed his police state against students, liberal intellectuals, and refractory pro-democracy clerics in 1999. Western Iran-observers largely followed suit, seeing the Khatami years as a brief, failed experiment in liberalization. Most Western commentators, especially those on the American Right, did not appreciate Khatami's relative "liberalism," his evolutionary importance, and how much the intellectual revolution that had elected him on May 23, 1997, terrified Khameneh'i, who for the first time probably realized his Islamic republic was in danger of rapidly evolving into "their" Islamic republic. In his very public prosecution in 1999 of Khatami's Interior Minister Abdullah Nouri, Khameneh'i revealed how much he feared change and first-generation revolutionary rivals who considered their credentials and accomplishments equal to his own. Like Mir Hussein Moussavi, Nouri could remember when Khameneh'i was a little man, put forth by Ali Akbar Hashemi-Rafsanjani, the real power at the time of Khomeini's death. Of no great clerical or intellectual status, who unlike Hashemi-Rafsanjani didn't enjoy Khomeini's affection and daily attention, Khameneh'i was supposed to be nonthreatening. His promotion to Khomeini's office was to guarantee a consensual leadership among the ayatollah's trusted lieutenants.

A disciple of both Khomeini and Montazeri, and an interior minister for Hashemi-Rafsanjani and Khatami, Nouri challenged Khameneh'i and the status quo by underscoring and mocking his fear of democracy and the United States.

Like Khatami but more aggressively, Nouri led the way to a democratic understanding of Islam, which has probably taken the high ground even among clerics. The brilliant and widely read reformist cleric Mohsen Kadivar, who has now taken refuge in the United States, may have best summed up a growing view among men of the cloth, especially among those who have grown to maturity since 1979, when he wrote:

> We can be religious in a way that allows us to obey all divine rules and dictates while observing those legal and natural rights of man that have been guaranteed by Islam. In areas where there are no religious dictates or prohibitions—and in my opinion most social, political, and economic, and cultural areas fall under this category—we can refer to the "legal conditions" of mankind. Many of the tenets of human rights that are being observed outside of Islam and Iran can be adopted in areas where religion is silent . . . We accept this rationality because it does not contradict our religion and is [in fact] necessary for our religiosity and Muslim identity.

This view has been even more powerfully stated by Mohammad Mojtahed-Shabestari, one of the older, most popular, and most renowned reformist clerics, who (so far) has not been driven into exile:

> I endorse democracy because it is the only system in contemporary times that allows mankind to reach the twin ideals of freedom and justice, without which humanity cannot fulfill its full potential and adequately perform its responsibilities before the Almighty. Only through free choice can mankind meet the full range of his responsibilities before God.

Mojtahed-Shabestari is notable for saying clearly what has become a dominant theme of the reformists, as well as the average Iranian complaining about the failures of the Islamic republic. He damns the "Islam of clerics" (*Islam-e foqahati*), which has bound the state to enforcing an antiquated, calcified understanding of the Holy Law. This refusal to modernize Islam's legal codes—to really wrestle with the contradictions and limitations that the law puts on basic freedoms in Iran—has perhaps fatally compromised the state and the clergy for many Iranians. More forcefully than any other mullah, Mojtahed-Shabestari, who was an enthusiastic admirer of Shariati in his youth, sees the country handcuffed to scripture. Part of the democratic solution to Iran's many problems is for the divines to exercise real, revolutionary *ijtihad*—new, innovative juridical reasoning that is both a right and an imperative for the leadership of the clergy. Mojtahed-Shabestari is actually at odds with a thousand years of Islamic legal process—the once generous theological disposition to not pry into a man's heart but only demand a common fidelity on the public square—that has become a lifeless, authoritarian orthodoxy in Iran. The 74-year-old cleric, educated in Qom, the country's seminary bastion, and in Hamburg, where he became the director of the Shia Islamic Center in the Imam Ali Mosque and grew comfortable with Western philosophers and ordinary Germans, wants Iranians to look for the historic religious essence of their faith, which rejects coercion. As Professor Kamrava succinctly put it, religious representative government has become for Mojtahed-Shabestari and other clerical reformers, "a necessity for Islam" and a "necessity for Iran."

Iran's democratic movement, perhaps above all else, wants to untangle what Shariati and Khomeini sought to irreparably bind together. The Green Movement is explicit in its desire to see greater—and among some of its most prominent supporters, complete—separation of church and state as a means of saving both. President Khatami was a never-ending contradiction in office, often incapable of defending his views or his supporters. But he unquestionably captured the dominant sentiment among Iran's youth, as well as most of Iran's millions of state employees, who overwhelmingly voted for him twice, when he wrote about what Iran should be:

> In this society, because man is who he is, he is treated with respect and dignity and his rights are observed. The citizens of Islamic civil society determine their own destiny and are in charge of their own affairs. In such a society the government is the people's servant and is answerable to them; it is not their superior.
>
> In our civil society, Muslims alone do not have the rights and privileges of citizenship, and, within the framework of the law, the rights and liberties of each person are protected and respected. I am not speaking of respect for human rights and civil liberties out of political considerations. Respect for human rights is an integral part of our religion and what Islam dictates.

In Khatami, the fire of Khomeini and Shariati has been extinguished. In its place is a love of progress. Although Khatami, unlike many in the Green Movement, still sees the world divided between Islam and the West, the virulent tension is gone. His much-praised "dialogue of civilizations" may have been more an argument for intellectual and technological theft from the West (we borrow from the West so that we can become the dominant civilization) than an argument in favor of brotherly love, but it is not a warrior's creed. Khatami wants to turn the page on Iran's violent relations with the United States. When he briefly erupted in anger in 2007 at Iran's not-so-clandestine support of death squads in Iraq, he revealed again his fatigue with Iran's dark revolutionary ways. For Khatami, like so many who populate the Green Movement, the Islamic revolution was supposed to transform man—first Iranians, then other Muslims, and then nonbelievers. Where once Khatami himself may have had a violent component in his faith (he would truly be the odd Iranian out if he didn't), his conception of the *insan-e kamil*, the "perfect man,"—which has been a powerful magnetic pole in Shiism's philosophical tradition and historical fuel for Iran's religious revolutionaries—has become more human (and Western) as Khatami has aged.

Post-Khomeini Iran's most influential religious intellectual Abdolkarim Soroush—probably the most important Muslim thinker since Hassan al-Banna (1906–1949), Sayyid Qutb (1906–1966), and Sayyid Abu'l Ala Mawdudi (1903–1979) gave birth to modern Islamic militancy—has also politely buried Shariati and the bellicose division of the world between believers and nonbelievers. For Soroush, who once may have drunk deeply of revolutionary Iran's violent, intolerant creed, a pluralist world is now the only moral choice:

> Epistemology, hermeneutics, historicism, religious experience, pluralism, spirituality, being in awe, reform, establishment, civil society, democracy, justice, citizenship, rationality, abandonment of ideology, and even replacing God as the protector of the dispossessed with God as compassionate and merciful all produce a new discourse that is serene and appropriate for the era of (postrevolutionary) establishment as compared to the combative and ideological discourse that was needed in the early phases of the revolution. The revolutionary discourse was needed then. Today calls for its own discourse.

Soroush is repelled by Islam as an ideology, which is to say, he is at odds with Iran's revolution and the still-dominant currents of modern Islamic thought in the Arab world. Soroush is a modern-day Al-Ghazali (d. 1111), the great medieval Muslim thinker who beat back the Greek philosophical challenge to traditional Muslim conceptions of God and revelation and, more importantly, made the widespread love affair with Sufism palatable to the clerical guardians of the faith. Al-Ghazali revitalized Islamic thought by legitimating Sufism's deep spirituality, which eventually consumed the Mongol invaders who traumatized Islamic civilization in the thirteenth century. Soroush has married Islam with democracy and eloquently established the intellectual basis for a secular democratic Muslim state that nourishes religion. Like many of the intellectual movers and shakers in Iran since 1989, Soroush is a great exponent of reason. A rational mind, according to him, does not negate the essence of any religion, which always speaks to man's mystical, supernatural needs. Reason can only better explain man's condition. An improving understanding of who men are, by science, historical reflection, and philosophical probing, cannot but improve man's ability to see his inner self, where the divine animates the soul.

For Soroush, everything is evolving. Evolution is both unstoppable and good. Progress is man's destiny and right. It should not be seen as religion's enemy.

> Religious knowledge—meaning our knowledge of the Qu'ran and the Sunna—is human knowledge, and, similar to other sciences, is in constant flux, evolution, and contraction and expansion. This contraction and expansion is directly produced by contractions and expansions in other areas of human knowledge, and understanding the Shari'a is not independent of our understanding of nature and science, and changes to it. Therefore, just as philosophy and the natural sciences are imperfect and continue to evolve, the sciences of jurisprudence [fiqh] and interpretation [tafsir] and ethics [akhlaq] and disputation [kalam] are also imperfect and . . . continue to

> evolve . . . Consistent with the growth of science and phi-
> losophy, the ability of scholars to expand and deepen their
> understanding of the Shari'a will also be enhanced.

Soroush, like many of post-Khomeini Iran's great intellectuals, now lives in exile in the United States. It is an irony
that he no doubt appreciates. However, Khameneh'i's Iran is
unlikely to be anymore successful in exiling dissident thought
than was the former Soviet Union. Before June 2009, even
the most senior members of the Green Movement probably
didn't have a good idea of how powerful their movement
would be after the election. Many members of the movement,
true to the intellectual honesty that has fueled dissident reflection since 1989, are quick to confess that they didn't see
the explosion that would happen after June 12. Like Khatami
in 1997, Iran's political opposition unquestionably underestimated the anger in the country. They underestimated themselves. After seeing the Green Movement gain force through
the spring of 2009, Khameneh'i didn't want to take another
chance of seeing 70 percent of the voters rally against
Mahmoud Ahmadinejad, the supreme leader's candidate. He
gave the order to rig the election, leaving in doubt whether
Ahmadinejad's zealous religious-nationalist populism really
has a popular base.

Khameneh'i's rash decision to throw the election to Ahmadinejad has compromised *all* future elections. He has permanently destabilized the country. National and municipal
elections—especially in the major cities—will now get post-
poned, perhaps indefinitely, or be so grossly controlled that
they can no longer be viewed by the regime as a legitimating
force (something not at all the case before the June 12 elections). Parliamentary and presidential elections have become

nitroglycerine. By the constitution and more powerfully by revolutionary practice, Khameneh'i cannot abolish them. Even when the Guardian Council, which has increasingly become an instrument of the supreme leader's unchecked will, was at its most aggressive in disqualifying candidates who could buck the system, elections in Iran held an element of legitimacy. Before June 12, the regime was just unable to disqualify everyone who didn't accept the status quo. There were too many big men of the revolution—men who were Khameneh'i's peers—whom the Guardian Council could not dismiss.

When elections occur now, Khameneh'i and his supporters in the Revolutionary Guards Corps will have to deploy massive force to the major cities, especially Tehran, the volcano of urban rebellion. With each election, tens, if not hundreds, of thousands of security forces may have to be deployed. Khameneh'i risks a spark, a violent action that provokes widespread public anger that could take the streets and test the faithfulness and fortitude of the Guards and their club-wielding cohorts in the Basij militia. With each election, Khameneh'i risks the reignition of a pro-democracy Green Movement, which, as in 1997 and 2009, could come out of nowhere to traumatize the state.

And Mir Hussein Moussavi, Mehdi Karroubi, and their supporters still show no signs that they intend to disappear even though the movement, as an organized opposition, has been crushed. With Moussavi in particular, Khameneh'i has created his own worst enemy. If Moussavi had won the election, he likely would have become another variation of an ineffectual Mohammad Khatami—except perhaps even less inclined to challenge the system. Unlike Khatami, Moussavi is not an intellectual—he did not have a developed political philosophy. He was a proud man with an unimpeachable revolutionary reputation, who had little regard for Khameneh'i. But he was not at war with the system. He is now. According to men who are close to him, he has had an epiphany. The regime has killed and jailed members of his family. Its thugs have threatened his politically active wife. He went to the urns and believes passionately that he won. He has irreversibly joined Iran's pro-democracy intellectual revolution that has been gaining ever-braver converts since 1989. It's a good guess that Khameneh'i believes that Moussavi will remain a serious threat to the regime survival until he's dead or locked away in Evin Prison.

Many Americans quite rightly ask what Iran would look like if the Green Movement, or its successor, had won. The answer isn't that hard to see: it would be democratic. How liberal? It's difficult to say. But the best bet is that any political system ruled by Iran's parliament, where candidates would compete freely, would likely be the most liberal in the Muslim Middle East. Religious conservatives would still have their sway in poor neighborhoods, but even here one can question how reactionary the vote would be. The Franco-Iranian scholar Farhad Khosrokhavar has done amazing field research in the holy city of Qom, headquarters for Iran's divines. In his book, *Avoir vingt ans au pays des ayatollahs* ("To Be Twenty in the Land of Ayatollahs"), which is a collection of interviews gathered over four years, Khosrokhavar paints a picture of a profoundly Westernizing Qom, where the young, especially young women, conceive of themselves as individuals endowed with rights, not just with obligations to God. The women seem almost Western in their belief that they—not their father, brother, or husband—should have the right to determine what they wear. They seem firmly attached to a romantic notion of love and marriage and are, more often than not, virulently opposed to the idea of polygamy, which is legal according to the Qu'ran and widely practiced among the older generations in Qom. Rare is the young woman or man who doubts the virtues of democracy or expresses a noticeable attachment to theocracy. According to Khosrokhavar, many of these youths were the children of senior clerics.

There is a difference in political opinion between the Green Movement's religious supporters and the secular reformers who want a clean separation of church and state. That difference could grow more hostile if the pro-democracy forces actually gained power. But in any tug-of-war, the secular side of the Green Movement seems more powerful. Iran's religious reformers—with the possible exception of the most faithful followers of the late Grand Ayatollah Montazeri—back a substantial separation of church and state. The religious and secularists could argue about when there should be some porousness between the two, but not about the basic need for separation. Khameneh'i has done his work well. It is hard to imagine the religious components of the Green Movement trying to abandon the democratic cause because hard-core liberal secularists, such as Akbar Ganji, who is contemptuous of the idea of democracy as a train running on Islamic rails, could gain too much power in parliament. However much pro-democracy dissident mullahs, who may represent a majority of the clergy, may loathe Ganji's kind, they have more in common with Ganji, who passionately believes in democracy, than the democracy-hostile and democracy-suspicious conservative clergy. And even among the conservative traditional mullahs, who have never loved Khameneh'i and retain considerable distaste for the autocratic theocratic system that Khomeini built, their opposition to change could be easily overestimated.

Iraq's Grand Ayatollah Ali al-Sistani, who is Iranian by birth and early education and is probably the most revered cleric in his birthplace precisely because he is a moderate, somewhat progressive traditionalist, has consistently made his preference known for secular politicians. He has unfailingly backed Iraq's democratic experiment; indeed, it would likely have perished without him. He gave his subtle but crucial approval of the American regency in Mesopotamia. His large following in Iran surely has something to do with his pro-democracy credentials in Iraq and his obvious distaste for Khameneh'i and Ahmadinejad.

Iran's senior clergy are unlikely to defy Khameneh'i before it is clear that the supreme leader's security apparatus has cracked. Montazeri was perhaps the last of the grand ayatol-lahs in open rebellion against the regime. But senior clerics, timid as they may be, won't likely stand in the way of change. The Green Movement, if it started to shatter the allegiance of the Revolutionary Guards (the only thing keeping it from power), probably would not be radically anticlerical. As with the Green Movement's message aimed at the Guards, its cler-ical message hasn't so far been hostile. The senior clergy could expect to have a soft landing in the new order. Funds would still flow from the new government to Qom. The Green Movement's young clerics would fan out to Iran's religious schools, explaining the value of cooperation.

And mullahs know how much the country has changed since 1989. The historic suspicion of the clergy—sublimely rendered by the poet-icon Hafiz Shirazi—has exploded under theocracy. There may not be an Iranian alive who now doesn't know these lines from Hafiz: *Va'izan kayn jelveh dar mehrabo membar mikonand/Chun be khalvat miravand an kar-e diger mikonand* ("From the pulpit, the preachers tell us how to behave, and then in private they do not what they preach.") The old Persian understanding, always most acidly expressed by faithful Muslims, that mullahs are always after sex and money, has become in the Islamic republic the dictionary definition of *akhund*, the now-universal pejorative to refer to clerics. The most consequential debates in the Islamic republic are no longer among divines. Famous clerical dissidents have certainly helped advance the pro-democracy cause, but laymen now hold the intellectual high ground. It is probably not an exaggeration to say that a majority of Iranians—perhaps a great majority—no longer care all that much what mullahs think about politics. As the conservative clergy feared from the earliest days of the revolution, power has despoiled the historic image of the *ulama* as the people's guardian angels.

Which brings us to the Revolutionary Guards Corps. The discussion of democracy in Iran often halts at their boots. Whatever changes have occurred in Iran mean nothing if the *sepah-e pasdaran*, as the corps is known in Persian, remains loyal. This is certainly true in so far as armed men will always defeat unarmed men if they are willing to kill in large numbers. While the post-Khomeini era for the Guards may have made the corps rich—the organization is estimated to own at least 40 percent of the economy—it has not ideologically reinforced them. Khameneh'i has superannuated—"purged" is a more accurate description—many within the first generation of the Guards. They, like Moussavi and Karroubi, remember Khameneh'i when he wasn't the supreme leader. Khameneh'i regularly plays musical chairs with those in power, reshuffling the hierarchy to ensure maximum loyalty. Westerners, who usually see corruption as antithetical with faith, make mistakes when they assess the revolutionary commitment of Iranian officials, who often lead corrupt lives. In Iran a fair amount of corruption can live side by side with sincere belief.

But there are limits. Members of the corps know how corrupt the institution has become. Like everyone else in the country, they hear rumors about the vast wealth of senior guardsmen. The regime depends on lower-class guardsmen, who do live better than the average Iranian. Service has its perks. But these young men are at the vortex of class resentment, which operates just as powerfully against the Guards now as it once did against the fabulously wealthy Hashemi-Rafsanjani, one of the most despised clerics in the country, and before him, the shah. It is wise to remember what membership in the Revolutionary Guards once meant: they were the country's protectors, the ultimate defense against the invader Saddam Hussein, the best Muslims of a proud revolutionary nation. They willingly gave their lives to defend the faith. They were poor young men who died by the tens of thousands. In life, they were heroes, in death martyrs. They were married to the charismatic Khomeini, the imam, in a supernatural way. They really did believe, as one *pasdar* wrote home to his parents:

> Do not worry about me. I don't belong to you now; I belong to God. We came into this world via the Almighty and we shall return to him. Don't you want to enter paradise as I will? Do not be concerned about my fate. . . . "To the triumph of the Islamic revolution under the direction of the Imam Khomeini!" I pray to God Most High to give the Imam long life and perfect health!

The *pasdar* died later in the war against Iraq.

For those who've met Revolutionary Guards members since the end of the Iraq War in 1988, this letter might as well be describing an alien race. To imagine young guardsmen dying happily to preserve Khameneh'i is surreal. They may, just possibly, die to preserve their jobs. They may even envision the corps as a special brotherhood—better Muslims than most (though this strains credulity given the wealth of their senior officers). They may fight out of fear for what might happen to them if Khameneh'i were to fall. But none of this seems solid.

The Revolutionary Guards Corps is—and still conceives of itself as—a religious institution, a brotherhood of holy warriors pledged to defend God's representative on earth (i.e., Khameneh'i). No doubt, many within the corps are still white-hot believers in the Islamic revolutionary cause, especially its war against the United States and Israel. Both the Islamic and Marxist sides of the corps' identity still reinforce its embrace of terrorism as a moral tool to defend and advance the dominion of God and his followers. But the Guards' actions have become irreversibly mundane. The charisma-free, insecure Khameneh'i has turned them into a mafia. The substantial anecdotal evidence suggesting that the guardsmen voted in large numbers for Mohammad Khatami makes perfect sense. They may have voted similarly for Moussavi, who had earned a good reputation among them during the Iran-Iraq War. They, perhaps more than anyone else, know how distasteful the system has become. Many in the Guards are educated men. Like the children of the clerics of Qom, they aren't immune to the intellectual revolution that has seized Iranian society since Khomeini's death. Are they really more loyal to Khameneh'i than the Iranian army was to the shah? Unless they've committed unspeakable crimes—and most guardsmen haven't—they may not fear democracy. Like the vast majority of their countrymen, they might actually like it.

The Arabs

How much does the past define us? Most Americans would answer "not much." Europeans, who still live in the shadow of the world wars, of castles and spiraling churches, would give more power to the past. But even with Europeans, the weight of history isn't what it used to be. Pick a major medieval battle, peasant revolt, or especially church council, and Frenchmen, Italians, and Poles would likely have a hard time relating how this event shaped them. To be a modern European is to rise above history, with its nationalist passions, abrasive cultural particularities, and especially its common but often divisive denominator of European identity: Christianity.

In the Arab Middle East, the dynamic is reversed. Classical and medieval Islamic history is more relevant today than it was in the 1950s, when Arab intellectuals generally downplayed the influence of the Prophet Muhammad, caliphs, and sultans on the modern, postcolonial Middle East. In great part, Islamic fundamentalism—the most energetic intellectual movement in the region since the 1960s—deserves credit for refocusing Muslim and Western attention backward. Not long ago, even well-educated faithful Muslims would have had difficulty locating Ibn Taymiyya (d. 1328), the renowned legal scholar of the stern Hanbalite religious school, in a general history of the evolution of Islamic legal and political thought. Thanks to contemporary Islamists, the medieval Damascene, who is often seen by today's holy warriors as their inspirational godfather, has become a household name.

Islamic fundamentalists may not have an acute grasp of the "glory that was Islam." Lovers of the faith's simpler Arabian days, they are hostile to the complexity that made "Islamdom," to borrow from the late Chicago historian Marshall Hodgson, the unrivaled urban civilization of premodern times. Today's Islamic militants like to highlight Ibn Taymiyya's distaste for illegitimate government and his affection for holy war; they do not dwell on other constant themes— his willingness to cooperate with morally imperfect sultans and his attention to weighing the costs and benefits of any action, particularly if violent.

Yet, their bad and selective history aside, Islamic fundamentalists cannot spiritually keep their balance without referring to the past, especially to its legal scholars and theologians, whom they cite to prove their contemporary arguments about the illegitimacy of today's rulers and the frightfulness of Western values. They operate on and exploit the widely held, and entirely understandable, sentiment among Muslims that God's intentions and rewards for his chosen people were clearer and more generous long ago than they are now. In the year 750, Arab Muslim power stretched from Portugal to China; today, with the exception of Turkey versus Greece, not a single Islamic state can claim military superiority over its primary non-Muslim rival. Even for the most historically insouciant, disbelieving Arab Muslim, this difference can be galling.

This contemporary love of the past, which is an expression of growing religiosity, is almost always seen by the West, and by many Westernized Arab Muslims, as an obstacle to progress. Devout Muslims, especially if they cross the poorly lit line into fundamentalism, are hopelessly antimodern to Western eyes. After 9/11, in countless conferences and articles, Americans and Europeans talked about the need to modernize the Middle East, where "modernize" was always a polite synonym for anesthetizing the region's defining faith. When the liberal writers Peter Beinart and George Packer confessed that they had supported the Iraq War (in Packer's case, apparently with considerable trepidation) in great part because of Kanan Makiya, the renowned Iraqi chronicler of Baathist totalitarianism and Arab intellectual decline, they expressed a widely held hope that Saddam Hussein's hideously awful Iraq could, just possibly, give birth to what the rest of the Arab world had not: some kind of liberal, democratic order.

Makiya was certainly aware that the process was going to be ugly because Saddam's rule had so savaged his homeland. Yet he, like many others, still hoped: if the right people could do the right things at the right times, then Iraqis (and Americans) might just make it. *The Atlantic Monthly*'s more neo-conservative Michael Kelly, who had written the finest first-hand account of the First Gulf War and viewed Saddam as a ferocious, depraved menace, and Paul Wolfowitz, the deputy secretary of defense, who was convinced that "moderate Muslims" were a silent majority throughout the Middle East, were not all that different in their hopes and aspirations in 2003. Iraqis were supposed to be the most secular of Muslim Arabs, perhaps the only positive by-product of decades of Baathist tyranny. Freed from Saddam, thankful Iraqi Arabs might even be able to do the unthinkable—help other Arabs to see that there were far worse things in this world than Israelis.

In 2003–04, when it became clear that Iraqi Arabs, both Sunni and Shiite, were no different from the other increasingly religious denizens of the region, despondency set in, especially among secular Iraqis who sincerely wanted to believe that their countrymen might somehow be different. Blaming Americans for the rise of religious power in post-Saddam Iraq has become popular among Westernized Iraqis. If the Americans had only done a better job militarily in 2003 and 2004, if they had only rejected the United Nations' advice to use a party-list system for elections and implemented a first-past-the-post single-member constituency electoral plan, and if they had only more forcefully chosen sides, then secularists, not religious sectarians, would have gained the upper hand.

And when Westerners discovered that Grand Ayatollah Ali al-Sistani, the most revered Shiite divine in the Muslim world and the best "moderate" cleric in Iraq, wasn't enthusiastic about Western social rights for women and was virulently hostile to homosexuality, they came to consider him spiritually intolerant, antidemocratic, and symbolic of a hopelessly retrograde region. In the eyes of *The New York Times* columnist Maureen Dowd, the fall of Saddam Hussein had egregiously set back women's rights—one more big reason why the war was a mistake. Many American women, and probably most liberals, would agree with Miss Dowd, which just underscores how distempered Westerners can become in assessing foreign societies that have not fully embraced "universal values," especially those about sex. Saddam Hussein's socially "progressive" regime, which gained more than a few admirers in the West for its advanced attitude about women's education, divorce, and nontraditional work, also was the first totalitarian state to regularly use rape as a means of political control.

Wherever Arab Muslims have shown themselves to be a bit too Islamic—for example, Gaza and the West Bank, Egypt, Algeria, Syria, Iraq, and Sudan—the Western reaction has been more or less the same: secularism has somehow misfired and produced more backward societies. And the dominant critique of this failure has usually been to suggest that more secularism, not less, is what is now required to save Muslims (and us) from the mess.

But what if this critique is wrong? What if progress in the Arab world overwhelmingly comes from the right, and not, as in the West and post-Khomeini Iran, from the left? What if to go forward, we must go "backward"? What if devoutly religious Arab Muslims, even fundamentalists, are more right about what ails their societies than we, enlightened secularists who have relegated the Almighty quietly into a recessed corner of our private lives, think possible? What if the path to political stability and basic human decency runs through the Holy Law and not—as most Arab regimes have thought since the region gained its independence from European imperialism and started implementing imported Western legal codes—around it?

What if the end of modern Islamic holy war among Arabs lies not in the spread of liberal freedoms and the triumph of modern Western ethics ("nothing divinely inspired is worth dying for"), but in the reinvigoration of much more conservative and mundane debates about Islamic ethics and how this religious school or theologian misreads the Shariah? Faithful Muslims see democracy not as we do, as a means to enhance and protect individual liberty and our secular space, but primarily as a way of creating a society that is more right-eous and likely to abide by the Holy Law.

But we should not merely assume that this conception of "Islamic democracy" is impractical or likely to do more harm to Arab Muslims (and us) than the dictatorships that have coarsened and intensified religious identity and mores. The answer to the Arab Muslim world's manifest problems may, simply put, be more Islam, not less.

In 2004 in *The Islamic Paradox*, I made the argument that when democracy arrives in the Arab Middle East, it will arrive via Shiite clerics and Sunni fundamentalists, and not via Westernized liberal Muslims or Westernized dictators fol-lowing in the footsteps of Mustafa Kemal Atatürk. That ar-gument seems sounder now than it did then. The religious forces in the Arab world have grown stronger; the liberals and their American supporters have grown weaker. The autocrats (for example, Egypt's Hosni Mubarak, the West Bank's Mah-moud Abbas, or Algeria's Abdelaziz Bouteflika), in whom some had put evolutionary hope, have not proven to be any fonder of real reform and representative government than they were when they first arrived in power.

The "realists" are probably right: the dictatorships of the Arab Middle East will likely continue, however unloved by the people below them. As long as the internal security ser-vices and armies can resist the subversive intellectual appeal and popular power of ever-more religious cultures, these re-gimes aren't going anywhere. When hard power hits soft power, soft power, at least in the short term, loses.

But religious legitimacy and popular approval do matter. Even the most avowedly religious regimes (Saudi Arabia and Iran), and even those with the most august royal bloodlines (Morocco and Jordan), have suffered from the same crisis of authority as have the secular dictatorships based on faded pan-Arab or more exclusive nationalist dreams (Egypt, Syria, Algeria, and Tunisia). The more modernized the state, the more severe this crisis has been. Most of these regimes have tried to incorporate some element of democracy into their political systems, however limited, because they know that representative government, even if just for show, must be part of the mix. In the past thirty years, they have all tried to enhance their religious legitimacy by drawing closer to or co-opting traditional religious authority or by embracing religious attitudes toward sensitive subjects (irreligious speech, apostasy, homosexuality, polygamy, and other issues revolving around female honor and behavior). Even the Baathist, heretical Shiite Alawite regime in Damascus has tried to get its creed redone as a more acceptable variation of Twelver or Imami Shiism, which is practiced in Iran, Iraq, Lebanon, and Bahrain.

These regimes see, even if many Westerners do not, that legitimacy in the Arab Middle East now springs from both God and the common man. Faithfulness to national socialism, dictatorial pan-Arabism, dictatorial Islamism, noble blood, or anti-Americanism and its obverse, Muslim-cum-nationalist dignity, isn't sufficient. The government of Hosni Mubarak tries just about everything—anti-Americanism, anti-Zionism, anti-Semitism, pan-Arabism, Egyptian nationalism, sympathy for conservative Islamic culture, greater space for the Shariah in Egypt's courts, more capitalism, and more socialism—and none of it seems to make his regime any more legitimate. If the spread of Islamic fundamentalism (measured by veiling among women, mosque attendance, the growing street and political power of the Muslim Brotherhood, and the solicitation of *fatwas* on both public and private issues) is a barometer of the regime's legitimacy in the eyes of the people, then Mubarak's presidency has seen a precipitous decline in support among both the masses and the educated elite. Mubarak's dogged persecution of fundamentalists and liberals who threaten his monopoly on power is also another good indicator that he is not at all sure of his popularity.

Muslim Middle Eastern regimes didn't amplify their democratic rhetoric in 2004 and 2005 just to appease George W. Bush. Given that the administration's rhetoric rarely matched its (punitive) actions, it is questionable how much Mubarak, Saudi Arabia's King Abdullah, or Tunisia's Zine al-Abidine Ben Ali feared an administration being humbled by Iraq. In all probability, these men underscored their democratic inclinations because they were unsure of their own populations: the Cedar Revolution in Lebanon, however briefly, captivated the Middle East as did the national elections in Iraq in January 2005.

The Middle East is, as always, an intellectual crossroads. When the Soviet Union and its European empire collapsed from people power and intellectual and economic exhaustion, Middle Easterners watched, some rejoiced, and some worried about the parallels (this was especially true in Iran, where Tehran's theocrat-controlled parliament nevertheless let loose some audible anxiety about the fall of unpopular dictatorships and important trading partners). When the Georgian Rose Revolution struck in late 2003, nine months after the fall of Saddam, and Ukraine's Orange Revolution struck one year later, Middle Easterners watched and wondered. Democracy dominated the public conversations. By late 2004, the region's rulers wanted to ride with, not against, the wave. That wave certainly broke, in part because President Bush's "Freedom Agenda" was always more rhetoric than muscle.

Soft power can have its successes—and the Cedar Revolution in Lebanon was, for a brief, glorious moment, aston-
ishingly successful. The United States and France, with the
"international community" behind them, and a big slice of
the Christian and Sunni Lebanese communities, who've always been the soul of their country's freewheeling, cosmo-
politan culture—all rhetorically ganged up on Syria's Bashar
al-Assad and his family's thugs who'd greedily plundered Lebanon for decades. For a moment, Lebanon's Hezbollah, who
both represent and terrorize the Lebanese Shia, were caught
off guard, uncertain of their Damascus ally and internal Lebanese chemistry. The idea of democracy in Lebanon has always been a sectarian mess, but that distracts little from the
fact that many Lebanese—perhaps even among the Shia—
wanted a government free of Syrian assassins and the unceas-
ing militancy of the Party of God. They naively hoped that
America and France might actually stand by them. Assad and
the Hezbollah once again have the upper hand. Killers, and
their apologists, are back in the saddle. But it's a decent bet
that if either Assad or the Hezbollah weaken, we will see that
the Cedar Revolution isn't as dead as conventional wisdom
now tells us.

The democratic ethic remains alive elsewhere. Just watch
Al Jazeera, the Qatar-based satellite TV channel, which is perhaps the most influential voice in the Arab Middle East. Al
Jazeera reflects well the modern Arab world's conflicted passions and preferences. It is pan-Arabist, Islamist, pan-Islamic,
anti-Western, anti-American (although deeply fascinated by
the United States), rabidly anti-Zionist (although not without
a sincere curiosity about Israel), and reflexively inclined toward gross anti-Semitism; and it has an enormous capacity to
portray, often worship, violence in its goriest details, especially

when the victims can be construed as martyrs for the faith and Arab pride. Al Jazeera lives on a diet of resentment, especially toward the West. The channel certainly has a blind spot for Persian Gulf sheikhs and emirs (unless they are Saudi), demonstrating that even die-hard Islamists and pan-Arabists know not to bite the hand that feeds them. Al Jazeera is relentlessly modern, yet usually reverential toward conservative religious figures (unless they are Shiite).

It is not, however, a voice fond of dictatorship. It may ally its coverage with despots against the Americans, as it did with Saddam Hussein. Its journalists have a very hard time separating the issues of kith and kin from larger issues of principle and evenhandedness (while Western journalism excels at self-criticism and glorifies "universal" principles over love of country, ethnicity, and God). Muslim Arabs rarely do this, at least in public. Nonetheless, Al Jazeera reaches out to democratic dissidents to an extent that belies just a provocateur's desire to cause trouble. The most famous democratic dissident in the Arab world, Saad Eddin Ibrahim, whom the Mubarak regime has repeatedly sentenced to jail for impugning the reputation of the Egyptian president, has been a regular guest on the channel, where he often argues in favor of the beneficent effect of former President Bush's focus on democracy in the region. The near mania that Al Jazeera has had for critiquing American neo-conservatism since 9/11, which is reflective of the Arab intellectual elite's firm belief in the power of American Jewry to dominate American society, betrays a fascination with the idea of democracy among the Arabs as well as an unhealthy focus on Jews. Al Jazeera journalists and guests generally see neoconservative support for democracy in the Middle East as a vehicle for pro-Israeli and neo-imperialist designs. Democracy among the Arabs, however, isn't damned, just what is seen as Jewish, militaristic, and Western imperialist machinations—that is, the need for the Arabs to have foreign, non-Muslim help—behind the cause.

The scholar who has probably watched more hours of Al Jazeera than any other Westerner, Marc Lynch, better known in the blogosphere under the pen name "Abu Aardvark," often sees a fairly strong pro-democratic bias at work in the broadcasts. There are many reasons why Al Jazeera gets under the skin of the region's rulers and maintains a broad following across the Middle East. The channel's sympathy for representative government and the vivid cultural debates that have mushroomed in the region as Middle Eastern societies have increasingly incorporated the combative, questioning ethics and style of the West are two big reasons why everybody watches it. Al Jazeera is popular because the channel is a virtual democracy for those in the Middle East who cannot yet have a real one.

The Middle East's great drama, which involves this collision and mixing of Islamism and democracy, and which so many in the West don't seem to know is taking place, can also be seen in the Arab media's coverage of Turkey, which has markedly increased since the country has become more openly Islamic under the influence of the ruling Islamist-sympathetic Justice and Development Party. Devout Muslims, who probably represent a majority of the population in every Arab land, have watched with growing curiosity the Turkish experiment with democratically elected Islamists. It is by no means clear where this experiment is going, but if the secularized Turkish army and supreme court do not close down Justice and Development (and one can easily share the anxiety of Istanbul's and Ankara's secular elite about the autocratic tendencies in the party), it may offer inspiration to the devout farther south who are seeing the region's most powerful secular society nevertheless offer the possibility that the faithful can democratically contest the supremacy of highly Westernized Muslims.

Whatever happens in Turkey, its experiment with Islamists, democracy, and republicanism is gaining speed and intensity. Post-Kemalist Turkey has irreversibly reentered the Muslim Middle East, vivifying the debate in the Muslim heartlands about the intersection of democracy, the Holy Law, and "Islamic values." Everywhere in the region where autocratic Arab regimes have experimented with elections— Algeria, Egypt, Morocco, Jordan, Kuwait, and Bahrain— Islamists have done well, probably winning the maximum number of seats that the regimes would allow them. This experimentation has certainly not shown the Islamist parties to be liberal.

Looking at these results and at the turnout in real elections in Iraq and the West Bank and Gaza, many Western observers have therefore concluded that the Muslim commitment to democracy is not viable, since in their view a sustainable, worth-dying-for democracy must by definition be more liberal than what has so far been seen among Muslim Arabs. If one cannot find Islamists who applaud the rights of man and place them above the duties owed to God, then one has not found democrats. Hence we have the common and growing Western critique of Islamic democracy that sees elections as the end of a democratizing process, not the beginning. The proper institutions and culture must be built first, so the argument goes. Whatever the West did from Runnymede until the foundation of true democracy in Europe and the

United States, Middle Eastern Muslims must somehow do, too, peacefully—before they hold elections.

For the Islamic-democracy critics, who span the political spectrum and count among them pro–Iraq War voices at the *New Republic*, the American Enterprise Institute, and the Washington Institute for Near East Policy, as well as a standard-bearer of more traditional conservatism such as George F. Will and a realist-cum-tepid-neoconservative such as Charles Krauthammer, it is unwise for the United States to encourage electoral politics in infertile Muslim lands where elections will enthrone America's enemies. These critics often decline to approve explicitly the regimes in place, and maintain their hope that more liberal Muslims can somehow become more competitive in conservative Muslim societies. But they are de facto saying that secular autocracies, regardless of their sins, are better than triumphant illiberal, devoutly religious "Islamic democrats," who hate America and American values and who, if they don't abort future elections once they gain power, will likely have pointless balloting since the diversity of views contested will be unappetizingly small. For these critics, with the accomplished historian Martin Kramer the most trenchant among them, democracy becomes the tool of Islamic extremism, not its antidote, as envisioned by President Bush.

But this critique badly misses what matters most. In the West, after (some of) its denizens started voting, it was the often-ugly evolution of democracy that built the necessary institutions that gave representative government real staying power. In the Arab Middle East, it may well be the "smallness" of the enterprise—the Holy Law–centered discussions— that gives roots to the democratic ethos among Muslims. The

French scholar Olivier Roy, who is not starry-eyed about the dark side of Islamic militancy, has put it well:

> It is clear that in the countries where the political game is open, if not democratic, the big Islamist movements are moderate and integrated (Turkey, Jordan, Morocco, Kuwait). Absolutely, the Islamists don't put their flags into their pockets. By definition, they do not renounce the idea that the law of God is superior to the law of men. But it is evident that democracy cannot be reduced to a consensus of values: it corresponds first to the founding of institutions that permit politics to remain open, no matter which party is in power. The path that [French] Catholics took with great difficulty— passing from their refusal to accept the Republic to a non-secularized Christian democracy—is open to Islamists. The question is not to sound out the "sincerity" of Islamists. Sincerity isn't a political concept . . . To speak of a "democratic culture" is a reconstruction of something that has already happened. Democratic culture does not precede democratic institutions; democratic culture is the internalization of these institutions.

Islam's "platoons" in favor of democracy cannot really be built, no matter the number of Western-financed micro loans to small businesses or the increase in Western aid to women's education, before Muslims go to the urns and get the opportunity to express their many values, often profoundly un-Western and anti-American. In Iran, the process of voting, as well as the innumerable failures of the Islamic revolution, have greatly aided the development of the Green Movement and a democratic culture in opposition to a theocratic state.

The Bush administration's enthusiasm for change among Arabs was extinguished by the experience in Iraq, by the victory of the Palestinian Hamas in free elections, and by the realization that the Egyptian Muslim Brotherhood, the mother ship of Sunni fundamentalism, would probably triumph in a free vote. Yet the discussion of reform, especially among the religiously devout, has attenuated little. Among fundamentalists in Egypt, as always a bellwether for where Sunni Islamists are headed, the interest in democratic politics seems to have gone up, not down, since the Bush administration ran out of pro-democracy steam in 2005. What needs to be better appreciated are the historical forces and philosophical ideas—from the earliest days of Islam—that make Islamic democracy the likely wave of the future.

Where I have previously emphasized the Westernization of Arab Muslims, especially devout Muslims, as a necessary and already quite advanced building block for representative government in the Middle East, this book goes the other way, emphasizing the historic components that will likely fuel and define the growth of democracy in Arab lands. Certain themes in Islamic history—the centripetal eminence of the Prophet Muhammad, the continuing quest for religious charisma, the recurring sense of failed expectations and justice denied, recurring rebellious violence, a profound sense of collective rather than individual identity and salvation, the tug-of-war between a clerically dominated religious establishment and popular faith, and the regularly battered but indefatigable power of the *ulama*, or learned scholars—are as important in understanding Islam's contemporary political possibilities as is the massive twentieth-century importation of socialist and fascist ideologies and all-enveloping "global" (American) values, which increasingly reshape and erase traditional Muslim sentiments, tastes, and ethics.

By going back in time, I will highlight why certain ideas and hopes—chiefly the slow evolution of a Western individualistic ethic, buttressed by a secular state ensuring religious neutrality in governance—are unlikely to have much support initially in the Arab Middle East and why the triumph of democracy in the region may depend upon their failure. I will not spend much time arguing that democracy will happen sooner, not later, in the region. Although I think it will be difficult for the Arab Middle East's autocracies to escape a democratic fate, dictatorships can obviously have staying power, even when their philosophical legitimacy is finished. With this said, Islamic history is no different from Occidental history: ideas matter. Regimes cannot sustain themselves indefinitely without philosophical legitimacy, and in the modern Middle East, most of the regimes have run dry. Hosni Mubarak rules but does not reign. The pan-Arabist Gamal Abdel Nasser, a nastier but vastly more magnetic dictator than Mubarak, ruled and reigned. There is simply no way Mubarak, or his son or a general who succeeds him, can revive or create a new legitimating idea for his dominion over the Egyptian people. Syria's Bashar al-Assad, Algeria's Bouteflika, Tunisia's Ben Ali, the Palestinian leader Mahmoud Abbas, and Ali Khameneh'i all have similar problems.

Democracy is the only serious, legitimate, political organizing ideal on the Muslim horizon, as more and more fundamentalists and autocrats realize. Some fundamentalists, particularly the extremists, may love the idea of a reborn caliphate, but in practice the faithful, at least in the most Westernized and urbanized Arab states—Egypt, Iraq, Algeria, Tunisia, and Morocco—have locked on to both the modern state as a point of loyalty (and, for many, love) and electoral politics as a vehicle for reforming society. It is increasingly popular in certain Western circles to compare Islamists to Nazis and Fascists, since the former would, so the suspicions go, use elections to gain power and snuff democracy out. All the polls in the Arab world that show an overwhelming preference for democracy over dictatorship really don't reveal what they claim, since the idea of democracy—or at least the Western idea of representative government—seems so poorly grasped. Democracy may be an appealing idea among many Arabs simply because it is the only conceivable way, outside a bloody revolution, that the old order can be overthrown. In this sense, sympathy for democracy now is similar to yesteryear's embrace of pan-Arab militarism in both cause and effect.

Compare Italian Fascists and German Nazis with the mainstream, election-winning Islamic fundamentalists in Algeria before they were crushed by the military in 1992, or the equally oppressed Al-Nahda movement in Tunisia, or the Muslim Brotherhood in Egypt. Among their many dissimilarities is the depth of their deliberations on representative government. We are not talking the Federalist Papers here. What happened in Algeria in the late 1980s and early 1990s, when the Islamic Salvation Front was born and briefly threatened the military junta that had ruled the country since the departure of the French, was overwhelmingly an expression of resentment and rage. But Algerians, however immaturely, started to think about democracy. Muslim public intellectuals have reflected more on the collision of the Holy Law and democracy than Western right-wing totalitarians ever did on the virtues of elected government. Absolutely there are undoubtedly Islamofascists in these fundamentalist movements, and it is a reasonable concern, based on what happened in Iran in 1979 and 1980, that the Islamist hard core could gain a choke hold on the more liberal strains of a democratic movement in which Islamists figure prominently. Nevertheless, the key here is evolution. In Iran, the democratic evo-

lution has been astonishing. The same circumstances—
principally a failed Marxist-Islamist revolution that has
provoked a massive wave of self-reflection (the dialectic turning inward)—don't exist in the Arab world. Even in Iraq,
where democracy has a toehold in society, we don't see the
same democratic passion that we've seen in Iran since June
12. The notion of communal ownership and responsibility,
masuliyat, or its obverse in Iran, outrage at the theft of a
controlled election, just isn't present yet anywhere in the Arab
world.

The Egyptian newspaper *Al-Masry Al-Youm* published in
August 2007 a version of the Brotherhood's first true political
platform, which was designed to help the organization gain
ground among the Egyptian people and, no doubt, introduce
more philosophical and political coherence to internal Brotherhood debates. The platform tells us the following:

> The Islamic state is a civil state, which means that political
> offices and roles are filled by elected citizens who are respon-
> sible through constitutional mechanisms for all conduct and
> behavior in governing [with the aim of] achieving the true
> popular will. The people are the source of authority [emphasis
> added], leading to the maintenance of society's security . . .
> Strengthening democracy requires conducting a comprehen-
> sive national dialogue, with the aim of boosting the confi-
> dence of the different groups within society, and agreeing on
> the rules of administering the political system and political
> work—an agreement that is far removed from the culture of
> exclusion. As a rule, it will be based on competition between
> political parties and forces, in accordance with the origins of
> political integration . . .
> Guarantees of Freedom: freedom has an Islamic and human
> heritage. It is the inherent principle in the contractual rela-
> tionship between citizens or different societal institutions on

one hand, and the governing authority on the other. It provides for equal justice among individuals and guarantees freedom of belief, . . . opinion, expression, movement, the press,
and formation of parties and associations . . .
Civil Society and Popular Institutions: the diversity and independence of civil society organizations is critical for both
the establishment of democracy and stability of the political
system. It is an interactive relationship that adds vitality to
social, cultural, and educational activities. Thus, facilitating
the establishment of these organizations and their independence is considered one of the general political priorities . . .

The Muslim Brotherhood is obviously an organization
trying to find its political center, and its members, like most
avowedly Muslim intellectuals, are often immature in how
they understand the complicated interplay of Western liberal
ideas and Western political institutions (a free press, an independent judiciary, a self-regulating legislature, an elected
but legally restrained executive branch). But these men—or
at least the younger members of the Brotherhood who drove
the production of this platform—certainly appear to be neither Ernest Röhm and the Brownshirts nor religious versions
of the American-supported secular autocrats whom the Islamists would like to replace. The Brotherhood appears torn between the older members, who have oscillated between an
evident distaste for democracy and democratic institutions
and a cynical use of democratic rhetoric, and the younger
crowd, who are probably a majority of the organization, who
have actually digested and like the idea of the Brotherhood
being tested at the urns. The above platform was issued, withdrawn, and then informally issued again—with the accompanying background commentary that serious divisions exist
among the Brothers about the merits of representative government—most likely because a real soulful tug-of-war exists

between the young and the old, between the *ancien régime* and those who believe the Brotherhood will never get the chance to govern unless Egyptians understand the organization is serious about more than one election.

We can easily find disturbing commentary and actions by many important members of the Brotherhood, or by the Justice and Development Party boss Recep Tayyip Erdogan, or Al-Nahda's intellectual guru, the Tunisian Rachid Ghannouchi, or the Islamic Salvation Front's guiding light Abbasi Madani. But we can just as easily find words and deeds, like the internal debate on and publication of the Brotherhood's (certainly imperfect) platform, which really ought to make us consider the possibility that these gentlemen are not liars, practicing *taqiyya*, religious dissimulation, waiting and planning to irreversibly acquire power. Rather, they are men who are religiously and politically evolving, marrying as best they can, sometimes in a highly contradictory manner, Islam and the West. They are trying to figure out how to take the best of the latter (material progress and the absence of brutality in daily life) without betraying the faith of the former.

This evolution isn't intellectually pretty, but these Muslims are trying to answer a need among the faithful, felt long and widely, to integrate the two civilizations and hence revivify their own. From the Salafist Muslim reformers of the nineteenth century, who tried to return to the examples of the Prophet Muhammad and his companions to find the intellectual means for Muslims to accept modernity, to the trailblazing religious dissidents of the Islamic revolution and the Islamic Republic of Iran (men such as Shariati, Soroush, Kadivar, Mojtahed-Shabestari, Khatami, and Nouri), the idea of a union of the best of the West and the best of Islam is behind all the intellectual tumult. Muslim intellectuals often do not pose the problem as such—one of the hallmarks of Khatami, the former president of Iran, is his willingness to admit that the West is sometimes morally superior to the Islamic world and that Muslims need to learn not just the technology of the West but also its powerful philosophical tradition, including ethics and epistemology, two touchy areas for believing Muslims.

These men absolutely do not love the West. They envy more than they admire. Yet they are not really at war with us, either. It should not be that hard to appreciate Ghannouchi's bitterness about the way many Westerners align themselves so easily with Middle Eastern dictatorships whenever devout Muslims enter the picture. It shouldn't be that hard to understand (though absolutely not condone) why some fundamentalists have turned to violence:

> The annoying thing is that when it comes to democracy and human rights, the record of the [secular Muslim] accusers plausibly leaves one skeptical . . . We are bathed in absurdity . . . They only accept the game of democracy on the condition that they are in every instance the winners. I will go further: suppose that we are inveterate anti-democrats, and that our adversaries are irreproachable democrats. They could, if they were sincere, constrain us to play the game of democracy. In France, the democratic sentiments of the extreme right (as those of the extreme left) are not evident, but no one thinks about excluding them from French democracy. The same for Israeli democracy or for democracy in America, Britain . . . It is thanks to the game of democracy that all the political parties nourished on authoritarian ideologies have been, in all countries, integrated, even . . . marginalized. So, if only to re-educate us, one should find a place for us in "democracy." There is (in Tunisia) a Communist party. No one asked them to renounce Marxism or defend Marxism as a democratic ideology in order to be recognized. In fact, only against us

do they brandish this requirement, because they want to get rid of a party that is strong and powerful.

Ghannouchi, Madani, and the primary players of the Muslim Brotherhood are all Muslim-Western hybrids. They may not be ideal representatives of a new democratic age in the Middle East. But those who would be ideal—liberal progressive Muslims—are vastly less relevant in Arab lands. Such Muslims—and the Egyptian sociologist and columnist Saad Eddin Ibrahim is the most famous and perhaps the most influential among Arabs—play well in the West and can prove themselves irritating to the Middle East's rulers. But they could not—*at least not yet*—win free elections.

In the mid-1980s, when I first arrived in Turkey, the Islamist slice of the electorate was hovering just under 10 percent (and most US officials in the country thought this was the fundamentalists' popular ceiling). The Islamist slice of the electorate now is probably somewhere between 30 and 40 percent if not higher. If we add those who are fed up with the more secular, Western political parties' cronyism and corruption and who are comfortable with their politicians openly praying at mosques and their wives wearing head scarves, we probably have a majority of Turks. Repeatedly, the Turkish military and the courts have gone after fundamentalists, banning their politicians and dissolving their political parties. This "proctoring" may well have obliged Islamists to evolve intellectually and spiritually. It has not damaged their popularity.

If we assume that Prime Minister Erdogan and other senior members of the Justice and Development Party are engaging in a democratic charade, waiting to accumulate the bureaucratic power to shred Turkey's explicitly secularist constitution (a legitimate concern given some of the party's actions), then it is surely a charade with which an increasingly large number of Turks are in sympathy. Those in the West and in Turkey who would like to see Justice and Development disbanded are essentially asking for dictatorial rule by an internally democratic, secular minority in the name of individual liberty, Western social values, and America's national security. If truly free elections were held in Egypt, Algeria, and Tunisia, we would likely see Islamist parties quickly develop a following that at least rivaled *Adalet ve Kalkinma*'s. The same might well be true, too, in Jordan and Morocco, where the tradition-loving monarchies are careful to give Islamist parties sufficient leeway to play politics, and thereby occasionally damage their popularity, but not enough freedom to ever challenge the regime electorally and thus honestly test the tribally based popularity of the royal families. The arguments against "rapid" democracy in all of these countries ("must not rush what took the West centuries; the common man culturally just isn't ready") are philosophically similar to the arguments that American and European conservatives once used to justify white-minority rule in southern Africa. (Black-ruled Zimbabwe is undoubtedly a catastrophe, and black-ruled South Africa appears to be a country in decline; in neither case is it easy, however, to imagine scenarios where the whites could have more slowly proctored black Africans into greater political maturity.) This position today against devout Muslims is probably morally unsustainable. Politically, it is a train wreck.

The Popularity of Islamic Fundamentalism among Arabs

Despite all the Western ingredients in its brew, Islamic fundamentalism is an authentic, deeply historical expression of Muslim anxiety and anger. Heavy-handed oppression, as we see in Egypt, Algeria, and Tunisia, or the much more light-handed harassment that we have seen in the Turkish republic, have only made the Islamist case stronger, not weaker.

What the central lands of Islam have experienced is a rediscovery of the need for some religious charisma in politics, either through men—whose learning, blood, good deeds, or "Islamic values" bring them closer to God—or through greater loyalty to the oldest charismatic element in Sunni Muslim life, the Holy Law. This charismatic impulse—a frequent occurrence in Islamic history when society is in shock, feels itself both threatened and more vigorous, and sees itself drowning in injustice—can lead to profound intellectual agitation and political mobilization (the Muslim Brotherhood today), and it can lead to violence, as it did with Ayatollah Ruhollah Khomeini and Osama bin Laden.

Contemporary Sunni extremists are expressions of the same spirit that led to Islam's first major and very violent splinter group, the Kharijites. They, like the Shia, who saw leadership belonging to Ali, the son-in-law and cousin of the Prophet Muhammad, and his descendants, established the principle that leadership of the Islamic community belonged to the most virtuous. Unlike the Shia, they saw virtue established by behavior, not blood. A branch of the Kharijites, the Azariqa, took this disposition to its logical conclusion and viewed themselves as the only true Muslims, that is, the only Muslims who were going to heaven; all others were "the people of Hell." "By thus excluding from the Islamic community even those Muslims who did not agree with them in every detail," wrote Edinburgh's William Montgomery Watt, "they made it lawful to kill such persons, and also their wives and children; for according to old Arab usage there was no wrong in killing someone not a member of one's tribe or an allied tribe, though it would be unwise to do so if the victim's tribe was strong." In support of and in reaction to the Kharijites and the Shia, who represent the other big and more lasting schism in Islam, the early Muslim community began to develop sentiments and doctrines about leadership and rebellion that still animate contemporary discussions. From birth—not just from the fall of the Ottoman Empire, as Osama bin Laden has suggested, or from the 1967 Six-Day War, when the Israelis demolished both pan-Arab and nationalist Arab pride—Islam has had a recurring legitimacy problem. As Princeton's Michael Cook has put it:

> Pre-Islamic Arabian society was tribal, and in considerable measure nomadic, inhabiting a land whose meager resources favored neither strong state authority nor elaborate social stratification. It was accordingly a society in which every man was an uncrowned king. Or to put it in more prosaic terms, political and military participation were very widely spread, far more so than in the mainstream of human societies— whether those of the steppe nomads, the later Islamic world, or the modern West. It was the fusion of this egalitarian and activist tribal ethos with the monotheist tradition that gave Islam its distinctive political character. In no other civilization was rebellion for conscience sake so widespread as it was in the early centuries of Islamic history; no other major religious tradition has lent itself to revival as a political ideology—and not just a political identity—in the modern world.

In times of stress, Muslims naturally seek God and try to find a vehicle for expressing his will. How can Arab Muslims try to establish legitimate government in the twenty-first century? It is probably fair to say that at no time since the early violent years of the faith have we seen a period when so many Arab Muslims have believed that they are living in an illegitimate era. For the most devout, this can be literally a question of salvation: how do they, as a community of Muslims, maintain their goodness—sufficient probity to get into heaven—when their rulers lead the community into sin?

When thinking about Islamic religious doctrine, it is imperative to remember that orthodoxy is orthopraxy: it is not what you believe, but how you (can) publicly practice your faith. What more and more Muslims in the Arab Middle East are saying—not just holy warriors like Osama bin Laden and Ayman al-Zawahiri—is that it is increasingly difficult to live as good Muslims under today's regimes. The so-called neo-fundamentalists, who try to avoid direct political confrontation with state power and to focus on social work and a religious renaissance at the grassroots level, have succeeded brilliantly throughout much of the Arab Middle East, transforming urban slums into communities of shared identity and common causes. Yet the injustices, especially the stark economic inequalities and the cultural distance between the ruling elite and the people, remain, becoming more unpalatable to the faithful as fundamentalism has become more mainstream and self-confident. For most devout Muslims, doing justice to the original divine inspiration and guidance of the prophet means respecting, to the extent that errant human beings can, the Sacred Law. The most-simple earthly signs of this growing commitment to spiritual renewal are the veil, increased prayer, and greater fastidiousness about *halal* (kosher) foods. But the commitment is also, unavoidably, political.

What we are now seeing in the Arab Muslim world—and it is certainly something we should want to see happen—is the "routinization" of this search for Islamic inspiration through the embrace of democracy. What we don't want to see happen is that today's profound sense of failure and injustice among many Arab Muslims produces an outrage in one extremely charismatic man, or in an elite theocratic vanguard; this is what occurred in Iran in 1978–79 and in a less convulsive, but still extremely deadly, way with Al Qaeda. This *Führerdemokratie*, to borrow a little crudely from Max Weber, is unlikely to happen again on a state level given the widely perceived unpleasantness and corruption of theocracy in the Islamic Republic of Iran and the egalitarian, cleric-leveling ethic in modern Sunni fundamentalism.

However, it isn't that hard to imagine circumstances in Egypt, where the Mubarak regime or an equally dictatorial successor attempts to crush the Muslim Brotherhood, producing an increasingly popular and violent resistance. Whereas the Muslim Brotherhood today wants to gain power through the ballot box, in the future, amid more violence and popular upheaval, we might see charismatic, crowd-rousing, and vengeance-seeking lay members of the Brotherhood gain the upper hand. If the army and the security services started to crack and these institutions are largely drawn from the lower social strata where the Islamic identity has skyrocketed, then we could see a variation of what we saw in Iran in 1978 and 1979. Given all the violence that has been generated in the name of Allah in the past thirty years, it is easy to understand the Western fear of empowered religion running amok among Muslims. It has inclined both Democratic and

Republican administrations toward the authoritarian status quo in the Middle East even though this status quo, especially in Egypt, keeps making the problem worse.

Both American liberals and conservatives, like Middle Eastern autocrats, have been hopeful that the raging debate among Muslim fundamentalists about Al Qaeda's sanguinary zeal, which has led to far more Muslims being killed than Americans or Israelis, signals the beginning of the end of Al Qaeda's appeal to the hearts and minds of young Muslims tempted to kill and die for the faith. This hope is probably well-founded. A consensus has developed among Arab Muslim fundamentalists that Islamic militants went too far in their embrace of violence in Algeria, Egypt, Saudi Arabia, and, most tellingly, Iraq. We can clearly see Muslims, who once easily condoned the slaughter of innocents as acceptable collateral damage in a righteous cause, wonder whether God will damn all those who kill believers, even infidels, in his name.

What hasn't been fully appreciated is that this fundamentalist reflection about God, man, and holy war is likely to reinforce the growing discussion about Allah, man, and the ballot box. Both discussions revolve around what actions make men and their societies righteous. For an increasing number of devout Arab Muslims, democracy is seen as the only means for returning Muslim society to a more virtuous state. Where secular dictatorships have sullied the community's mores, democracy will aid religion and allow more virtuous men to lead society.

This essay is not an apologia for Islamic conservatives and militants. The cultural and social views that sprang from the Muslim Brotherhood in the 1920s, even when viewed in the context of the anti-imperial sentiments from which they emerged, are not views that a Westerner can esteem. And in some ways, Muslim fundamentalism has gotten uglier since the 1920s. In sync with modern times, many religious Muslims are now willing to tolerate, sometimes condone, the murder of both non-Muslim and Muslim women and children if the cause is right (which usually meant, before the Second Iraq War, killing Americans, Israelis, or just Jews in general). Today we see a regular stream of female suicide bombers, where not that long ago even the most hard-core holy warriors recoiled from using mothers, sisters, and daughters as instruments of war.* I have no intention of sugarcoating the cultural foulness and bigotry that we can find so easily among today's progressive Muslims, let alone among fundamentalists. (Dinner parties with the conspiracy-afflicted Egyptian, Saudi, and Jordanian secularized elites, for example, can make Noam Chomsky look nice, introspective, and analytically even-handed.)

Yet I don't believe this ugliness will likely prevent Middle Eastern Muslims from establishing successful democracies where governments arrive and fall, repeatedly, via the ballot box. In 1900, France was rife with the worst hatreds that

* The good news here is that Muslims, let alone Americans and Europeans on YouTube, have started to deploy savage humor against this phenomenon. Such humor in the Middle East, often as vivid among the religious as among the secularized, ought to tell us that ethical deliberations are alive, if not well. A parallel between today's modern Sunni holy warriors and the Kharijites of old is again possible to see in their use of women in combat. Although it is clear that the use of women as warriors today stems overwhelmingly from the Westernization of Muslim men, a juxtaposition is still interesting: as the Kharijites moved toward "mainstream" Muslim society, their radical views became embarrassing and were discarded. Among the practices discarded was the use of women as *jihadists*. Today's Kharijites have been more successful in exporting their beliefs and tactics to the center. The massive slaughter of Shiite women and children by Al Qaeda in Iraq seems to have finally caused the mainstream to recoil in disgust.

Europe had managed to produce; but France was unquestionably a democracy, not as estimable in conduct and character as some Frenchmen then would have liked, but a real democracy nonetheless. As Olivier Roy has aptly written about his country, "If we had to wait for everyone to become a democrat before creating democracy, France would still be a monarchy."

The Past as Present:
Charisma, Community, and Salvation

For Westerners, whose modern history is largely about decoupling God and politics, little about Islam and democracy makes much sense. Our basic understanding of justice, personal and political moderation, individualism, and representative government is about emphasizing the epistemological uncertainty of metaphysics, most specifically how one man can never trust the communication between another man and God. No one really has the right to preach about what the Almighty intends since no man is more exegetically talented than any other. Unlike the Qur'an, the Bible is not the literal word of Yahweh, the Father, the Son, or the Holy Ghost. Muslims once had a protracted, intense debate on whether the Qur'an was "created" or had always existed in time, only to be called forth by Muhammad; Jews and Christians have never similarly debated the historicity of the Bible.

As the great works of the Latin and Greek fathers of the Western and Eastern churches amply point out, Christianity never really had an interpretative hierarchy of priests and laymen that inspired much unity. Jesus through the centuries is constantly changing, although constants about his character remain, in particular his emphasis upon divine love and redemption. As a cultural and political force, he is as varied as the art that depicts him. The church may have stood in the way of the Enlightenment, but Christianity, given its evolution and perhaps its core beliefs, just proved incapable of withstanding the onslaught of the Renaissance and the rediscovery of the Greeks. If the historian Charles Freeman is right, once the church-state alliance of the late Roman/early medieval period started to crack, and the Greeks' insidious inductive reasoning again began to take the intellectual high ground, the Western mind was destined to pound to pieces— or, to put it more politely, reshape—Christian self-confidence and the idea that men and their imprecise languages can receive and convey a divine being's commandments. The privatization of faith and the slow withdrawal of religion from the public square were, among other things, defense mechanisms to ensure that Westerners didn't become completely godless creatures.

Similarly "reshaping" Muslim self-confidence is a much more daunting task. Unlike Jesus, the Prophet Muhammad isn't soft. From the Umayyad dynasty, which succeeded to the caliphate after the death of Ali (he was assassinated in 661), the fourth and last of the "Rightly Guided" caliphs, to the resplendent Abbasids of Baghdad (750–1258), to the ferocious but culturally exquisite Timurids of Transoxania and Persia (1370–1507) and the heterodox Persian-Turkic Mughals of India (1526–1858), and finally to the Ottomans, who produced the most European of Islam's great empires (1281–1924), the prophet remains a constant even though Muslim culture changes enormously. He is neither the messenger of a private faith nor really a guide to individual redemption. He is, as the late William Montgomery Watt described him, a man of two personalities but one mission. There is Muhammad at Mecca, the often tremulous poet, searching for and fearing God's inspiration, and Muhammad at Medina, the rising ruler of a conquering faith. Both Muhammads are united in their quest to create a community, a state, of believers through both divinely inspired moral suasion and force. Muhammad's offer of salvation is communitarian. Although his vision of God's grace and the nonbeliever's perdition revolves around each individual's voluntary choices, Muhammad is always focused on the community of believers as a living body, a reflection of God's will and (as Muslims start to win on the battlefield more than they lose) God's military might.

By comparison, Jesus is a more intimate, almost feminine figure. Thus the enormous struggle within Christianity between the Nestorians, who emphasized Jesus' humanity, and the Monophysites, who emphasized his divinity. Even when Christ was most awe-inspiring, under the early Holy Roman Empire, a Christian could take his spirit into a corner of an abbey or chapel, or alone into an open field, and quietly seek communion. Solitary monks contemplating their sinful souls and Christ's love seems natural to us still and certainly seemed right to Christians of the Middle Ages. Even a religiously eclectic Sufi mystic, the closet thing Islam has to a monk, just doesn't do this with the Prophet Muhammad (but he can do this with both Jesus and the Virgin Mary, who are often seen by Sufis as Muslim apostles of love).

Muhammad is easily the most successful charismatic figure in history. Moses led the Jews out of Egypt and established the Jewish identity; building upon Moses, Muhammad inspired the Arabs and propelled them to conquer and convert the richest and most intellectually productive region of the planet. Except for the most chiliastic Shia, who elevate the Caliph Ali into an unrivaled thaumaturge, the prophet for

Muslims is the reference point for everything. Christianity is premised on Jesus' death and resurrection; Islam is premised on the prophet's life. The centripetal weight of Muhammad on Islamic history just cannot be overstated. When Islamic militants and ordinary Muslims protested Western caricatures of the prophet or, most violently, Salman Rushdie's literary play on the Qur'an's famous "Satanic Verses," they were rising to the defense of the most important element in their religious identity, which is the most important thing that faithful Muslims have. Such protests against infidel actions are new. Why Muslims today care about what non-Muslims say about them is a fascinating, quintessentially modern change in attitudes (and, all in all, a hopeful sign, as I will explain). But it was entirely natural that "globalized" Muslims would respond in the way that they did.

The Qur'an is not a comprehensive guide to the Islamic faith and is no more valuable than the Bible as a lens to understand its faith-based civilization. But it isn't metaphysically as flexible a document as are the Gospels. In the Qur'an, duties, expectations, and divine promise are sufficiently specific and concrete that every believing Muslim to this day has some understanding of how he orders his life, his society, his home, and his inheritance from this book. No one text could possibly handle the myriad legal questions of an evolving, geographically immense, and culturally varied religious community, which is why, in part, the schools of Islamic jurisprudence, *fiqh* (which literally means to "understand" or "ascertain"), came into being to fill the void.* These religious

* The Shariah is a preordained legal system of God's commandments. Legal scholars and judges do not make law; they ascertain it through a variety of approved methods. The differing legal schools approve of different analytical methods for trying to ascertain what would be the appropriate, God-approved judgment for any legal question.

schools, however, came to increasingly limit, not expand, what we in the West call "positive" law.

After the death of the prophet, the caliphs retained the founder's ability to promulgate new, divinely guided legislation. As Patricia Crone and Martin Hinds have convincingly shown, the caliphs through the coming of the Abbasids viewed themselves, and were probably viewed by many of their followers, as the guides and gatekeepers to paradise. Their authority came directly from God, not vicariously through the Prophet Muhammad. They were, in Arabic, the *khalifat Allah*, the "deputy of God," not the *khalifat rasul Allah*, "the deputy of the messenger of God." However, this authority was challenged on several fronts, most effectively by a cadre of lawyers who came to be recognized as the '*ulamâ*, which means "those who know." They insisted that caliphs were below the Holy Law and that even divinely ordained rulers had to ascertain what the law was through consultation.

This process culminates with the work of Muhammad ibn Idris al-Shafi'i (b. 767), the most pivotal figure in Islamic jurisprudence. According to the late legal scholar N.J. Coulson, Al-Shafi'i "appears on the stage as the deus ex machina of this time, who seeks to unravel the tangled threads of multiple controversies and propound a solution to create order out of existing chaos." Al-Shafi'i recognizes the Traditions of the Prophet, the collected oral histories of Muhammad's statements, as "a source of the divine will complementary to the Qur'an." This is the "supreme contribution of al-Shafi'i to Islamic jurisprudence," according to Coulson, and it effectively puts the final nail into the coffin of the caliphs' juridical independence from the religious scholars, who are the custodians and interpreters of the traditions. Henceforth, the *ulama* had the most important keys to religious and thus political legitimacy. In the words of Crone and Hinds, "the historically significant point is that a ruler who has no say at all in the definition of the law by which his subjects have chosen to live cannot rule those subjects in any but a purely military sense . . . Rulers were obeyed as outsiders to the community, not as representatives of it . . . The state was thus something which sat on top of society, not something which was rooted in it . . . From the point of view of the political development of the Islamic world, the victory of the *'ulamâ* was thus a costly one."

Reinterpreting the prophet, taking him and his traditions out of seventh-century Arabia—or as modern Muslim reformers would like to do, respectfully keeping him in the seventh century and applying his wisdom, but not all his literal injunctions, to modern times—has thus been very difficult. Al-Shafi'i's victory has held like a rock: the *ulama* as a group have never been in favor of reform since it runs against their conception of the divine order and their own power. This is why, in part, individual Muslim reformers have struggled, so far unsuccessfully, with devising some means of reinterpreting the Qur'an and the traditions so that the desired modern, usually very Western, answers could be devised. The tendentiousness of it all has often been too much to bear, except for Westernized Muslims whose primary objective has been to figure out some way to be Muslim in name but Western in spirit and practice. These Muslim reformers have often been attacked for being the carriers of "imported ideas," a deadly insult among fundamentalists and sometimes among less devout but still very proud Muslims.

The Arab Ulama and Reform

Throughout the modern period, the *ulama* in most countries have been able to keep a certain distance from those who rule. This was easier during the 1950s and 1960s, since most secularizing rulers in the Middle East wanted little to do with clerics, who were seen as hopelessly atavistic. However, when the rulers came calling, as Nasser did in Egypt, the clerics did what they were told. Since the 1970s, the *ulama* who have drawn too close to power have often been outflanked by other clerics, sometimes informally educated without deep instruction in the traditional religious sciences, who are closer to the people and more radical. In the past, ecumenically inclined Sufi preachers were neighborhood sages. But popular religion today is dominated by small-mosque prayer leaders (imams), often educated on Saudi stipends, and by more distant TV and Internet divines. The television evangelist and well-schooled cleric Youssef al-Qaradawi, who has authorized the slaughter of Israeli girls (since they are the future mothers of Israeli soldiers) by suicide bombers and approved modestly attired Muslim women playing soccer, has probably become the most influential Sunni legal authority thanks to al-Jazeera. Officially supported Sunni clerics, not blind to their diminishing flocks, have as a result generally increased their distance from today's unelected presidents and kings. This tendency is perhaps the most noticeable in Egypt, where the crisis of legitimacy for the Mubarak regime is acute and the pro-elections Islamist opposition is the most organized and powerful.

What needs to be understood in all of this is that any legitimate form of government in the contemporary Arab Middle East must be seen to be complementary to the Prophet Muhammad's legacy and the Holy Law. Islamic history ought to tell us that any secular system that makes a frontal assault on the clergy has virtually no chance of gaining sufficient popular support to be deemed legitimate. (The Iranians, who've lived under theocracy, are much more "evolved" about clerics, the prophet, and the Holy Law.) The *ulama* can certainly be pushed and pulled, but only legitimately and most effectively by their dissatisfied flock, not by their overlords. The religious scholars in Egypt, as elsewhere in the Muslim world (with the possible exception of Iran, where pro-democratic clerics are on the cutting edge of dissent), are a conservative force fearing change.

Yet it is a decent bet that if Al-Azhar were free from state control, its scholars would incline more toward the Muslim Brotherhood's position in favor of more representative government than the Mubarak regime's current compact with the religious establishment, which allows the clergy more input into culture in exchange for political quiescence.

Iran's dictatorial clergy offer an illuminating parallel. The senior clerics of the regime often tie themselves into linguistic knots to avoid saying the obvious: they, not the people, rule. The hard core of the regime—like Ayatollah Mohammad Taqi Mesbah-Yazdi, the so-called spiritual adviser to Iran's President Mahmoud Ahmadinejad—will damn democracy directly, but most don't. The landslide victory of Khatami in May 1997 and the June 12 presidential election in 2009 allowed many within the clergy, if only briefly, to come forward with more pro-democratic sentiments. The brutal way the regime persecuted Khatami's interior minister, Abdullah Nouri, the outspoken pro-democracy clerical disciple of Khomeini, suggests strongly how sensitive the regime is to clerics who want more power to the people. The importance and busyness of the Special Clerical Court in Iran, which tried

Nouri, and the massive deployment of security to the holy city of Qom after June 12 hints at the number of clerics who don't like the dictatorship implemented in their name and at the distance that has developed between the cleric-despising but still faithful population and the mullahs. Iraq's Arab Shiite clergy can talk endlessly about the lessons learned from the Islamic Republic of Iran. And the Sunni *ulama* have little of the Shiite *ulama*'s sense of separateness and self-confidence. It is no secret in the Sunni Arab world that Iranian mullahs are not much beloved by their flock. The odds are high that once Sunni Muslims start to vote en masse, the Sunni *ulama* are not going to tell them that democracy is irreligious and that religious scholars have an unquestioned right to veto parliamentary legislation.

The Western and Westernized Muslim hope that secular regimes would produce a self-sustaining "neo-*ijtihad*" movement, where modern clerics backed by modern, autocratic secular governments would reopen "the door of *ijtihad*"—the right of Sunni Muslim jurists to exercise independent (modern) judgment—has not panned out. For a time, Western observers and scholars, and certainly Westernized Muslims who had married themselves to the region's modernizing regimes (and who were the West's primary interlocutors in analyzing their societies) hoped that this "neo-*ijtihad*" movement would allow Islamic law to align itself with modern (Western) standards and sentiments. The Islamic world, too, could have its own Laurence Tribe.

Yet if we read the commentary of Islamic modernists from the 1840s to the 1940s—probably the Middle East's most liberal age, because it was nourished, if not also oppressed, by France's and Great Britain's liberal imperialism—it is impossible not to see the arrestment of a sincere Muslim attempt to mix liberal Western ideas into Muslim history, especially into the methods of juridical reasoning used to "discover" the truth in the Holy Law. This process was essentially aborted by the more "progressive" Arab nationalist dictatorships that took power in the Middle East in the 1950s and 1960s. The more organic give-and-take of an earlier time, when men of sincere, reforming faith could attain high office and influence—for example, Rifa'a Rafi' al-Tahtawi (1801–1873) who must be reckoned modern Egypt's most enlightened thinker, the Circassian slave who eventually became Ottoman Grand Vizier Khayr ad-Din al-Tunisi, and the renowned Egyptian intellectual and judge Muhammad Abduh—dies in the more thorough Westernizing era that starts in the 1950s, when autocrats dictate the creation of more modern men and women. Society is ordered to transform itself. For a time, in certain quarters, it does. Slowly but surely, however, the Muslim bedrock counterattacks through an increasing attachment to its Islamic identity.

In the modern world, the only way to restore peacefully a more organic relationship between those who govern and the rest of society is through the ballot box. Arab Muslim communities, with due attention to national differences, will likely move toward this end as communities, not as a collection of individuals allied by their selfish interests (the Madisonian-American way). From the beginning, Muslims identified themselves as an *umma*, a community, sought salvation together, or were damned together if their caliphal leadership failed them. The communitarian disposition—the need to separate the world ethically between believers and nonbelievers—is still enormously strong. Democracy offers the possibility for the *umma*, as a community, to ensure that a majority of Muslims, a quorum for the holy if you will, cannot be seriously attacked by religious or secular extremists unless the extremists are willing to endure permanent exile from the community. (A condition that few members of Al Qaeda probably would want to endure.)

This does not mean at all that democratic Muslim politics will not be afflicted with faction. It will, of course, and we can only hope that faction complicates the political objectives of devout Muslims as much as it frustrates Democrats and Republicans in the United States. But in the beginning, we will probably see fundamentalists operating as they did in Algeria before the military junta crushed the democratic experiment in January 1992, and as they do today in Egypt— that is, as a mini-*umma*, emphasizing their common ground, not their differences.

This is a major reason why Muslim fundamentalists, from Morocco to Iraq, are increasingly in favor of elections. Democracy, with the Shariah's family law and "values" center stage, is, as Grand Ayatollah Ali al-Sistani of Iraq regularly reminds us, the only viable principle for motivating believers as a group. It is not at all surprising that Sunni Islamic democratic ideas are probably the most advanced in Egypt and Algeria, given the profound Westernization of both the Muslim Brotherhood and Algerian Islamists and their deeply held faith in an idealized Muslim community.

There is certainly trepidation, distrust, and even loathing on the part of many fundamentalists for the democratic process. Osama bin Laden and the Algerian militant Ali Belhaj criticize democracy's presumption to put man, not God, at the center of existence; this is an old, and entirely logical, assessment of what democracy could do to the Islamic universe. In the West, under democracy, religion isn't safe from devastating attack, and Muslim intellectuals, even ensconced in dilapidated concrete row houses without running water in the Iraqi holy city of Najaf, can be aware of Western scholars who have applied unbounded curiosity and rigorous analytical methods to the sacred historicity of the Qur'an as if it were a lamb in a butcher shop. Such things do scare, because many fundamentalists believe in a slippery slope—just like Americans who think that if Islamists get a toe in the governing door, they will eventually seize their societies and convert them to religious dictatorships.

But this fundamentalist fear of sliding is a sign of real, perhaps imminent, progress: the critiques are so vivid since antidemocratic fundamentalists know well the growing intellectual appeal of democratic politics in the Middle East. They watch Al Jazeera. They hear the internal debates of the Egyptian Muslim Brotherhood. They see the Turks—the damned Turks!—move in the direction of an Islamist-tolerating democracy. They watched Iraqi Shiites—damned Shiites!—by the millions turn out to vote in 2005 and 2010. In the provincial and national elections of 2010, millions of Iraqi Sunnis also voted. This time around, the Sunnis decided that it had been an error to shun the elections of 2005.

Osama bin Laden and his more intellectual cohort, Ayman al-Zawahiri, are so savage about democracy among Muslims, especially Iraqi Muslims, because they know what this means: the end of an ethical order where their violence makes sense. Now, Bin Laden and Al-Zawahiri can reach back in time to many rebellious theologians who depict a virtuous Muslim community being led astray by impious rulers. Let them try to do that when Muslims are voting en masse in the big Arab states. What will surely happen to them is the same thing that happened to the Kharijite extremists of early Islam: the Muslim community exiled them, killed them, and in-

clined them to evolve philosophically. As Bin Laden and Al-
Zawahiri are historically sensitive holy warriors, the parallel
has probably already occurred to them.

A Troubling Future

What will Arab Islamist democracy look like? Imagine a more
socially conservative version of what would likely be the case
in a democratic Iran. Although it is difficult for many Americans to accept a complementary Iranian parallel, it is not a
bad one. Take away the Islamic republic's clerical overlords,
and Persian democracy could probably be both vital and religious. And thirty-one years of theocracy have done wonders
for removing religion from the deliberations of what officially
is called an "Islamic parliament."

We can expect the same process of effective secularization
to occur inside any Islamist-dominated Arab legislature,
though probably more slowly since a real democratic exchange
among devout Muslims may keep government more religious,
not less.

Many of the ethical debates that will occur inside any
fundamentalist-heavy Arab parliament will surely make Westerners recoil in disgust, especially on issues related to family
and sex. But even here, we should not get too depressed too
quickly. Again, let us look at Iran. Although Arab Muslims
in general tend to be more socially conservative than their
Iranian counterparts (and this is especially true for Iraqi Shiites), the discussions about family and sex that occur inside
Iran, which operate under severe censorship, are still pretty
sensitive to both Western criticism and internal Iranian criticism, which has become deeply permeated by Western values.
The clerical regime in Tehran hates being seen as anti-women,

and will contort itself to show that the Islamic republic has created a society that guards "female virtue" and offers women the opportunity to advance educationally and professionally. The latter point is a by-product of Iran's Westernized mores; it is not even a consideration in traditional Islamic societies. If it were not for the regime's dictatorially mandated rules against women, Iran's female-majority population would have probably wreaked a good deal of modernist havoc through a freely elected legislature. Let us remember that Khatami would not have won the presidential election in 1997 without the votes of women. The Green Movement probably would not have taken off without angry women driving it. It was not the fault of these women, who were clearly pushing for substantial political and cultural reform, that Khatami proved so impotent in confronting the ruling, all-male establishment, or that the Revolutionary Guards Corps has not yet been overcome.

In September 2007, the students at Columbia University missed a golden opportunity to engage Iran's current president, Mahmoud Ahmadinejad, in a meaningful debate when one of them asked him about homosexual persecution in the Islamic republic. Ahmadinejad was obviously flummoxed by the question—homosexuality just isn't something that most Iranians recognize publicly as a legitimate part of society. The ethics behind contemporary Western rights for homosexuals are in a different moral universe, or to put it differently, are further down the ethical evolutionary road that Iran is already on. Talking about women's rights, however, is well within the boundaries; and for Iranians, as well as Egyptians, Algerians, Tunisians, and Iraqis, it is an unavoidable subject because so many women now have to work outside the home. Fundamentalists are always talking about women, and we should, in turn, always talk about them when talking to fundamentalists. The entire moral order for Islamists revolves around female honor. They need to confront women's issues head on, preferably inside of parliaments where they must openly argue their case with veiled and unveiled women staring at them.

Democracy will be taking hold in traditional, modernizing Arab Muslim societies when we see debates that for us seem to be misplaced in a legislature, or just too primitive to take seriously. A healthy Islamic democracy will surely discuss textual considerations involved in interpreting the Qur'an and the Holy Law. What had in the past been the domain of judges and scholars in religious schools—assessing the relevance and value of the Traditions of the Prophet, and in the case of the Shia, the Traditions of Ali—could well become the domain of legislatures, particularly in Sunni Arab lands where the organization, prestige, and soft power of the clergy is vastly less than among Shiites. Parliamentary concern about such issues could fuel a healthy give-and-take between the elected representatives of the people and the faith's traditional guardians—the type of organic growth in debate about law, society, and religion that has been all but absent during the pan-Arab and Arab-nationalist post–World War II era. It could well fuel the much-dreamed-of "neo-*ijtihad*" movement and the reformation of the religious sciences.

As the liberal Islamic legal scholar Khaled Abou El Fadl has argued (echoing the views of Mohammad Mojtahed-Shabestari), Islamic discourse needs to move away from its modern authoritarian traditions (think the Saudis) and rediscover the more tolerant and competitive attitude that existed when Sunnism, as a corpus of legal thought, was being formed. Democracy is, if nothing else, a competitive political system, whose jousting ethos permeates everything else in society. Westerners should not want to see Islam's classical schools of law and their religious sciences buried in the archives of the Middle East's mosques and sterile madrasas. We want to see them revitalized: Hanafis versus Malikis versus Shafi'is versus Hanbalis (especially the Hanbalis who are close to the Saudi interpretation of the faith) versus the Shiite Ja'faris. We want to see them argue, as they once did, that no one can represent or embody the divine will, that, as El Fadl puts it, "human knowledge is separate and apart from the Divine knowledge." We want to see Islam's contemporary theologians invoke the historic Muslim jurist's warning: *Allahu a'lam* ("God knows best"). Man's foremost moral and legal duty is thus to guard himself against error and ignorance, to resist the hubris that through *fiqh*, the study of the Holy Law, any man can exclusively know God's order. Modern autocracies in the Middle East have suppressed such philosophical debates, as they have suppressed so much else.

Parliaments, once they get going, have a way of looking upon themselves as supreme. Legislatures, not clerical schools, are likely to be the most decisive forum for the great ethical debates, especially among Sunni Muslims. One of the open questions for any Islamic democracy is how Muslims incorporate their religious scholars into ethical and legislative deliberations. In Iran under the mullahs' tyranny, clerical oversight of the political process is total. In Iraq and Lebanon, where democracy is taking root or holding on, clerical oversight of legislative issues is informal with no constitutional protection. Iraqis who care about what Grand Ayatollah Ali al-Sistani thinks solicit his opinion; or Sistani offers it on those issues that compel his commentary. The same was true for the late Grand Ayatollah Mohammad Hussein Fadlallah, the Iraqi-born spiritual leader of the Hezbollah and much of the Lebanese Shiite community. (He was born in Najaf, but to a clerical family that hailed from southern Lebanon. He made his way to Beirut in 1966.) Either man could conceivably trump elected officials—Sistani has now done so on a few occasions. But it happens only because Sistani enjoys a charismatic authority that Shiites voluntarily bestow upon the most elite religious scholars, who have through decades of studying the Holy Law acquired an aura that is both very human and a bit unworldly.

But it is already apparent in Iraq that Sistani and the other senior clerics in the holy city of Najaf understand that politics is a double-edged sword. If they invest themselves in a project or an opinion, and it doesn't turn out as well as hoped, they can get blamed. Shiite clerics, even more than the pope, survive by the love and awe that they inspire in believers who are entirely free to turn away from them. No Shiite cleric, not even Ayatollah Khomeini when he was overcome by human waves of adulation, ever arrogated to himself the power of Gabriel standing at the Pearly Gates.

In any free Shiite society, senior clerics will have moral authority that could be deployed in elections and parliamentary debates. Westerners, who find this idea an unacceptable affront to proper democratic practice, would do well to remember that in the modern Middle East, as in Europe, it has been laymen inspired by the promise and power of modernity, not religious men defending traditional ethics, who have wreaked the most havoc. Intellectually, we are held hostage by the memory of Khomeini. The great danger in Iraq is not that the holy men of Najaf will have too much influence in Baghdad, but that they will have too little.

Unlike the Shiites, who have been thinking seriously about the proper role of clerics in earthly governance for one hundred years, the Sunnis have yet to figure any of this out, in large part because they have had no opportunity to really try. (Iranian and Iraqi Shiite divines had their first chance in the 1905–11 Iranian Constitutional Revolution.) The Islamic Salvation Front never got far philosophically and programmatically before the Algerian military shut down the democratic process in 1992. Nevertheless, we can see that members of the Front and other Islamic groups in Algeria were trying to work out intellectually, if not bureaucratically, some means to assess religious questions as a political movement. It certainly appeared that the development of a religious hierarchy was unlikely. The Front's most prominent and influential members were lay public intellectuals, which is the case with most Sunni fundamentalist movements. Sunni Islam's lack of a universally recognized clerical hierarchy, or even an informal means of ranking one cleric's opinions above another's, has produced a chaotic collection of religious schools and issuances of opinions (*fatwas*) by Sunni divines. Moderate and militant Sunnis have the same problem, though with the more militant, the issue is even more chronic because the disputatious disposition is more intense, the regard for "proper" schooling is low (it produces clerical toadies), and the egalitarian instinct ("your *fatwa* is no better than mine") is strong. In the summer of 2010, King Abdullah of Saudi Arabia shook the Sunni world when he issued a royal decree restricting the right to render *fatwas* to the kingdom's highest clerical body, the Council of Higher Ulama. The aim, it was understood, was to put an end to the chaos that issuing *fatwas* had become.

In Egypt, the Muslim Brotherhood's political platform—
the first really in its history—provoked considerable contro-
versy in the country among members and supporters of the
Brotherhood and especially in the Coptic Christian community, because the first draft of the platform contained refer-
ences to a religious oversight body that would judge the content of legislation passed by parliament. The idea was
withdrawn. Although Cairo has the Al-Azhar establishment,
which is probably the most influential religious institution in
the Sunni world, the Brotherhood is certainly not Al-Azhar.
How the Brotherhood would—if it actually could—organize
a supervisory body for the Egyptian legislature is as unclear
now as it was before the Brotherhood first published its platform. This certainly shows that democracy is an acquired taste
and that not all the members of the Brotherhood want to let
Egyptians have full rein. A powerful strain in Islamic thought
is that humans have many bad impulses, especially libidinous
ones, and they need to be constrained by the law.

The famous Qur'anic dictum *al-amr bi'l-maruf wa an-
nahy an al-munkar* ("commanding good, forbidding evil") is
about this fear of unconstrained human appetite, and it runs
against modern Western sentiments in favor of expansive
individual freedoms. This injunction, however, does not pre-
clude democratic government. In the past, Western legislatures and local councils often enacted draconian moral codes,
many of them with more punitive bite than what the Islamic
world actually meted out to people of unconventional habits
and pleasures. The democratic idea is carrying the day within
the Brotherhood because (i) it is the only alternative to dictatorship and (ii) more and more Muslims see democracy as
a vehicle for enshrining a faithful consensus. "Islamic values,"
whatever they are, are thus better protected. This view is enor-

mously strong in Iraq among the senior clergy in Najaf, who appear to believe quite firmly that the majority of Iraqi Muslims are good Muslims and that a democratic Iraq has to be a more moral place than what has come before (a reasonable conjecture).

Through the democratic process, the Egyptian Brothers, like all other Arab fundamentalists, will get to discover "Islamic values." If the majority of Egyptian Muslims repeatedly votes one way, it is a very good bet that the Brotherhood, always sensitive to public opinion, will discover that commendable Muslim values overlap rather well with Egyptian voting patterns. The Sunni clergy's conservative historical ethos has usually bent to authority and especially popular consensus. The medieval clergy strongly disliked Sufism, but reluctantly accepted it when it became too popular to condemn and once the great theologian Al-Ghazali successfully blended it into orthodoxy. Sufism in its many medieval incarnations was often wildly heterodox, pushing the envelope of recognizable Islamic practice and belief. Accepting democracy into "traditional" Islamic dogma will likely be easier than the *ulama*'s slow acceptance of Sufism, which still makes many clerics recoil in disgust. If Arab Muslims want to vote for their leaders, and the evidence in the highly Westernized and urbanized countries—Algeria, Tunisia, Morocco, Iraq, and Egypt—is that they clearly do, the clerical establishment is unlikely to fight a rearguard action against it. In Iraq we've already seen Sunnis massively abstain from one national election (2005) and then, realizing their mistake, massively vote in 2010 for a political coalition led by the secular Shiite Ayad Allawi. Iraq's Sunni clergy, many of whom were energetically discouraging the vote in 2005, were hard to detect five years later. The overtly religious Sunnis did poorly in the most recent municipal and national elections. A consensus has already developed in the community that their men of religion, though not without influence, are not pivotal. As in Iraq and probably elsewhere, Sunni Arab legislatures likely will not have severe competition from their respective clerical establishments. Whether this is good or bad for healthy debate inside government and among the chattering classes is an open question.

The Turks

Ne Mutlu Türküm Diyene! These words—"How happy I am to be a Turk!"—have been the unofficial pledge of allegiance. Wherever you find a statue or picture of Mustafa Kemal Atatürk, the World War I general who willed a Turkish republic out of the ruins of the Ottoman Empire, you're likely to find it. Both an order and a wish, it encapsulates Atatürk's ambition: his children, proud holy warriors who once terrified Christian Europe, were to become just Turks—a nation with Western dreams rendered in a Latin alphabet.

But the political elite of the Justice and Development Party no longer dreams like the country's founding father. Since 2002, it has been the dominant party in Turkish politics. Under the leadership of Recep Tayyip Erdogan, the AKP, as the party is known by its Turkish initials, has enthusiastically sought to reintroduce religious themes and values into government and culture. Where once many Westerners believed that Turkey's secular dictatorship would gradually give way to the first liberal democracy in the Muslim world, today some observers hope that Turkey can become *the* democratic model for devout Muslims. A more religious and democratic Turkey might compromise some of Atatürk's most sacred dreams. Turkey may become a profoundly anti-American, anti-Israeli, and anti-Semitic country. But the country could develop a more competitive, healthy political system, where faithful and secular Muslims vie for the country's soul in free elections.

But then again, AKP could take the country the opposite way, uprooting the fundamentally liberal institutions and culture that finally allowed AKP to win elections. It is always much easier to destroy than build, and the party's achievements so far—outside the economy where they would make Milton Friedman reasonably proud—give cause for considerable concern. Although one can make good arguments for why a more democratic but anti-American Turkey is still better for the United States than a recognizably pro-American authoritarian state (democracies in the end do make better allies, besides being vastly more humane to the citizenry), it's still an open question whether AKP's type of anti-Americanism and anti-Zionism contain within it such a virulently antiliberal streak that it could compromise Turkey's democratic evolution.

Vali Nasr, the academic-turned-State Department adviser, wrote a book in 2009, *Forces of Fortune*, that argues that growing capitalism in the Middle East will produce a large Muslim middle class that will be both vigorously faithful and more determined to establish and maintain representative government. Applying Max Weber's *The Protestant Ethic and the Spirit of Capitalism* to Muslims, Nasr sees the Justice and Development Party's Turkey already as a successful democratic model, which could well provide an alternative to faithful Arabs hunting for more moral governance and political freedom. There is certainly something in Nasr's argument, which plays off the observations of Samuel Huntington. But there is also the undeniable fact that capitalism and fascism can cohabit pretty well, as "Communist" China and the Third Reich amply prove. (Capitalism in the twenty-first century may finally get China, but right now Chinese enterprise is making the country vastly more powerful but not correspondingly free.) The passivity of Nasr's argument—we just have to be patient—is certainly comforting to American officials. It encourages, however, outsiders to be blind to the dark side of Turkish Islamism.

Far more aggressively than anyone in the Arab world or among Europe's anti-Zionist denizens, Prime Minister Erdogan has worked to spread anti-Israeli anger. Drive along Istanbul's vast new automated highway system and you'll see a stunning array of anti-Israeli poster art. Istanbul's bookshops, long holding a small nasty anti-Semitic subculture, have become cornucopias of anti-Jewish literature. State-supported Turkish "moderate Islam"—which is present in hundreds of mosques and religious schools throughout Europe and Central Asia—could well become conduits for radicalization. There are many reasons why Turkey's overseas state-supported religious institutions have not become notable incubators of radicalism, but certainly a big one has been a certain distaste among religious Turks for provocative politics (more on this later).

If a radicalized Turkish Islam were to marry itself to the causes of the Egyptian Muslim Brotherhood, for example, the mother ship of Sunni Arab fundamentalism and the Palestinian radical group Hamas, we could see the transference of the worst instincts and aspirations of the Brotherhood to Turkish Islam. The Justice and Development Party, like its Islamist Turkish predecessors, has had worrying ties to Saudi Arabia, which has helped fund the explosion of mosques and religious centers throughout Turkey. Twenty-five years ago when I walked the rundown, religious neighborhoods of Fatih in old Istanbul, I could already see the influence of Saudi money— Saudi-financed mosques looked so much better than those financed through local donations and the Turkish state. (Interestingly, religious Turks who didn't like the Saudis subsidizing their faith were quick to tell foreigners all about the donation system that brought Saudi cash to the Golden Horn.) Wahhabi instructors informally could be found throughout Istanbul, always rumored to be in the country as guests of the religious wing of the ruling Motherland Party (its boss, Turgut Özal, attracted under a big tent many devout Turks who otherwise would have made their home with Necmettin Erbakan, the founder of the fundamentalist Welfare Party, a forerunner of the AKP). In a more militant Turkey, where state religious institutions, especially the large religious foundations (the *vakif*), are either part of an explicitly proselytizing government or are freed of the state entirely, as the AKP wants them to be, Turkish Islam could become an incomparable engine of anti-Americanism, anti-Zionism, and anti-Semitism. The terrorist potential of this shouldn't be discounted.

When the Islamic identity rises in a country, and it's been politically ascending in Turkey for at least thirty years, a Muslim-versus-non-Muslim mentality inevitably follows. (The Qur'an, the literal word of God, is a monotheistic powerhouse: it presents a bipolar world between virtuous and struggling Muslims and everyone else who isn't being helpful to the cause.) These sentiments were vividly on display in the AKP's semiofficial sponsorship of the pro-Hamas Gaza-bound flotilla that Israeli commandos stopped in May 2010. Anti-Zionist sympathies have been strong in the die-hard secular Turkish Left for decades. When I served in Turkey with the

CIA in the 1980s, it was not uncommon to meet young Turkish diplomats, who didn't have a religious bone in their bodies, revile the Jewish state. But left-wing, anti-Zionist officials would never have so provocatively aligned Turkey with Palestinian Islamic militants, or for that matter, Arabs of any stripe. (The Turkish Left on this issue parts company with the European Left.) Erdogan's exuberant backing of Ali Khameneh'i's nuclear position against the United States and UN sanctions and the AKP's profound queasiness, which will likely turn into hostility, toward the Obama administration's plans to partially base an anti-Iranian ballistic missile defense shield in Turkey are also clear signs that Turkey's political and cultural identity is changing.

The Justice and Development Party's more Islamist forerunner, the Welfare Party—created in 1987 by Erbakan, who served as Turkey's first Islamist prime minister from July 1996 to June 1997, before being banished from power by the Turkish army in its first peaceful, just-a-few-tanks-on-parade, "postmodern coup"—was much more explicit in its desire to see Turkey turn away from the West toward the Islamic world. The time of the Islamists had not yet come; Erbakan was no match for the secular elites in the army and the judiciary. A prominent member of the Welfare Party, Abdüllah Gül, who briefly became prime minister and then the AKP's hard-charging, pro-European Union foreign minister (2003–2007) and is now the country's president, once famously remarked about Turkey's European and Muslim identities: "We don't want to be the last of the foxes. We want to be the head of the sheep."

So which is the real Abdüllah Gül? The English-speaking, English-educated Ph.D. who wants Turkey to be part of the European Union, a club of Christian and post-Christian secularists who would self-righteously intrude in many profound ways into Turkey's national sovereignty and Muslim identity, or the one who wanted to turn toward the Islamic world? Turkey's current Foreign Minister Ahmet Davutoglu, a German-speaking Ph.D. in political science and international relations, has long been the AKP's foreign affairs theoretician. He is the über-neo-Ottomanist. Taking a page from Edward Said, Davutoglu thinks Turks have been held hostage by Kemalism and Western scholarship on the Middle East, which has made Turks view the Ottoman Empire and the Arabs negatively. Davutoglu wants to liberate Turkey intellectually from the West, to reverse what the Turkish-speaking former CIA official Graham Fuller has colorfully described as "the Kemalist historical lobotomy performed on the Turkish public," and develop a "friendly neighbor" policy toward the Arabs and the Iranians. Davutoglu is probably the mastermind behind Turkey's support to the intercepted Gaza-bound flotilla; he may have had a hand in the post-flotilla propaganda campaign toward the European Union in Brussels, where Turkey's representative passed out informational packets containing pictures of ultra-Orthodox Jews protesting Israel's existence. His men can regularly let you know that Ankara likes dealing directly with Barack Hussein Obama, always emphasizing the president's middle name and his Muslim ancestry, and not the assistant secretary of state for Europe, Philip Gordon, who is, they let you know, Jewish. Like Erdogan, Davutoglu hasn't renounced Turkey's bid for EU membership. He might aggressively seek it if the Europeans gave Turkey a renewed signal that they are now serious about the admissions process.

Are Gül and Davutoglu schizophrenic? Are they, as many secular Turks and their Western allies suspect, just deceptive, seeking EU admission as a means to guarantee that the Turkish army doesn't pull off another "postmodern coup" while never really wanting membership in an intrusive, morally decayed European order? Or are Erdogan, Gül, and Davutoglu just evolving in confusing, contradictory ways? A new-age Turkish Islamist with neo-Ottoman aspirations could well envision Turkey in Europe (the Ottomans were at the gates of Vienna twice), while being at one with the Arabs and the Iranians and being deeply suspicious of Americans and virulently hostile to the Israelis. The AKP *is* a work in progress. With Turkey finally becoming an economic dynamo, in great part because of the AKP's embrace of free enterprise, and the statist Kemalist order giving way, the Erdogan government knows it is venturing into uncharted waters. These are men who can probably remember that twenty-five years ago Turkish Islamists weren't all that much different from the militants in Algeria's Islamic Salvation Front or Egypt's Muslim Brotherhood, who really did believe *al-Islam huwa al-hall* ("Islam has all answers"). It wasn't the Turkish army that then kept these men from power (although the army probably saw it that way); it was Turkish voters.

As the AKP's religious stance on domestic politics has softened and become more nuanced, which is also true for its foreign policy (twenty-five years ago Turkey's Islamists uniformly thought the EU was Beelzebub), Turkish voters have backed the party in ever increasing numbers. Although the AKP has lost a number of early supporters among the Turkish intelligentsia and the Istanbul business establishment, their profound unease has yet to translate into voter dissastisfaction with the AKP. Now, it is possible that the AKP's evolution could reverse as the party becomes more powerful. Omnipresent stories about new alcohol restrictions in the cities and towns of central Anatolia, the AKP's economically dynamic power base, are distressing because they strike at the heart and reality of modern Turkey, where mosques and bars, even in small towns, haven't been far apart. (I haven't personally verified these anti-alcohol stories; old-time Kemalists often believe as gospel just about any story that suggests that a more Islamic Turkey is on a slippery slope to hell.) As mayor of Istanbul, Erdogan did try to make the city more "moral," which meant, among other things, greater obstinacy about issuing and reissuing liquor licenses. (He was mostly beaten back by Istanbul's die-hard beer and raki drinkers.)

According to former Turkish intelligence officials, Justice and Development has done a surprisingly good job of taking control of the Turkish national intelligence service, the *Milli Istihbarat Teskilati* (MIT), from the Kemalists who long dominated the organization. With MIT and the national police in AKP hands, the secular Istanbul business community, which has become increasingly hostile to Prime Minister Erdogan's strong-arm tactics, is scared to voice too loudly its criticisms of the prime minister and his party. The MIT, much like the French and Italian internal intelligence services, and the Turkish national police have long loved intercepts and wiretaps, using thousands of them each year against the state's enemies and those deemed suspicious. When I was visiting Istanbul in 2009 and 2010, longtime business friends were visibly nervous about saying anything critical of the AKP on the phone. The Turkish government's multibillion-dollar tax-evasion prosecution of the Dogan media group, which is the most independent and AKP-hostile media conglomerate in the country, has certainly reinforced the fear that critical voices in the business community will be severely punished. Female TV news and media celebrities have told me that they've come under pressure to be more conservative in their appearance and cautious in their commentary about Islam. Turkish Radio and Television, the state-owned media organization, certainly appears now to be a tool of Justice and Development (which is not too dissimilar to TRT practices when secularists governed). Turkish print journalism, which has struggled to develop standards of integrity (the Turkish press has generally been deeply ideological in its allegiances, conforming more to the European model of advocacy journalism than the American ideal of fact-based, politically neutral reporting), appears more cowed by the AKP than it ever was in the 1980s and 1990s by the military. A few of their columnists aside, *Hürriyet* and *Milliyet*, the two big secular newspapers of the center and center-right, now appear to be towing the AKP line. And a vibrant Islamist press and private media companies have developed since 2002, which so far have not shown a penchant for turning on their own.

And then there is the profound influence of the unusual Islamist-Sufi Gülen movement, which is the largest and richest religious movement in Turkey and in the Turkish diaspora in Europe. For Turkish secularists, the Gülenists are upsetting because they have been effective in melding "Islamic values" with Turkish nationalism, especially within the national police. The Gülen movement may have actually helped to make the Turkish police a more cohesive, honest organization, which for years under various secular governments has been riddled with corruption and often mixed up with Turkey's powerful crime syndicates. (Ankara's desire to join the European Union has also encouraged the national government to get the country's police forces, which would often beat people in detention, under control.) The movement's head Fethullah Gülen—who lives in Pennsylvania, and probably came to America in 1998 to escape the surveillance of the Turkish military and possible prosecution for advocating, in the view of the army, the creation of an Islamic state—has established a global religious movement aimed overwhelmingly at Turkic-speaking peoples, with elementary and middle schools, universities, social services, libraries, and youth clubs as part of his master plan to rebuild Muslim society from the ground up. Gülen's philosophy of Islamic activism revolves around three broad ideas: service to country and community, self-sacrifice, and temperate reflection married to persevering will. Gülen's critics would add at least one other element: *takiya*, a Sunni variation of Shiite "deception," where true views are hidden for self-preservation and ultimate triumph.

The Gülenists are what French academics would describe as "neo-fundamentalists" as they explicitly reject political organizing and focus on grassroots conversion of the Muslim faithful to their cause. They are explicitly modernist in that their movement aims to adapt traditional Islamic values to modern life, although it isn't always crystal clear what this adaptation entails. Gülen has always been in favor of veiling on women, and his movement, like all Islamic movements, is deeply concerned about the sexual freedom that comes with Westernization. Like Sufism of old, the movement has done well with the poor and the rich, the uneducated and the college crowd. The movement has gained admirers in odd quarters. For example, the former Iraqi defense and finance minister-turned scholar, Ali Allawi, who is no admirer of Islamic fundamentalism, views the Gülen movement as one of the few bright spots in contemporary Islamic thought. Gülen personally seems free of the crude anti-Zionism and anti-Semitism that increasingly permeate AKP policy, speeches, and highway art. He was reportedly deeply disturbed by the pro-Hamas flotilla, putting more blame on the flotilla's promoters than on the Israeli commandos for the violence that ensued.

Unlike the typical Arab Sunni neo-fundamentalist movement, the Gülenists are not at odds with the state or the army, which the movement has always treated with considerable public deference and respect. The Turkish officer corps, on the other hand, views the movement as a serious threat to Kemalism and regards its overt politeness and social agenda as a deceptive, underground effort to topple Atatürk's legacy. Among the secular upper crust of Istanbul and Ankara, the Gülenists are probably seen as the most dangerous religious movement in the country—far more dangerous than the more militant Sunni groups that fertilized the growth of the AKP's more explicitly Islamist predecessors. Even among Turks who know the United States well (not a large crowd), one easily finds incredulity about why Washington has allowed Gülen to live in Pennsylvania, from where he orchestrates his religious empire.

The fear of Gülen has undoubtedly grown because Prime Minister Erdogan has been, so far, effective at co-opting and humbling two great pillars of Kemalism—the Istanbul business community and the army. And he is on the verge of humbling the third pillar of secularism, the judiciary, through a constitution-changing referendum. Some of Istanbul's wealthiest secular families, who rose to prominence in the Kemalist era of close state-business cooperation (the Sabancis and Kochs are the most famous), still remain friendly with the AKP, whose business-friendly policies have unquestionably contributed to extraordinary growth in the country. The Turkish secular business elite in the 1980s were rich; now they are superrich. Attitudes among secular businessmen toward Justice and Development are changing, however. The tax prosecution of the Dogan media empire—one fine in September 2009 was $2.5 billion, almost four-fifths of the market value of Dogan Holding—has spooked businessmen. I have met numerous members of TUSIAD, the Turkish Industrialists' and Businessmen's Association, in Washington, DC, and in Brussels, expressing in private their growing reservations about the Justice and Development Party's political intentions.

But Prime Minister Erdogan has reserved most of his anger for the Turkish military. He has struck at it hard through the prosecution of what is called the *Ergenekon* case, taking what may have been a theoretical training exercise for a coup against Islamists and turning it into a judicial witch hunt to intimidate and humble the military. This alleged military conspiracy, which was supposed to culminate in the government's reversal before 2010 and which AKP supporters refer to as the "*Ergenekon* terror organization," was officially revealed in the summer of 2008. State prosecutors have jailed hundreds of military officers and their civilian "allies"—and questioned hundreds more—and filed charges that beggar the most conspiratorial imagination. The so-called "deep government" of right-wing, die-hard Kemalist officials no doubt exists in an informal way: Turkish officialdom, like the old Istanbul business elite, is clannish and inclined toward intermarriage; Kemalism among many military officers is a sacred ideology where democracy and civil rights are ancillary ideas to uncompromising secularism and, among some older military officers, loathing for anything Islamic. But it is doubtful that any large conclave exists where Turkish generals and colonels, in cahoots with Kemalist journalists and academics, methodically plot against this elected government or its predecessors. (For no other reason, it's operationally sloppy.)

It is conceivable, though just barely, that the army would attempt a coup against the AKP. After the attempted so-called "e-coup" of April 2007—when the Turkish General Staff's official website posted a warning against the AKP ("certain circles . . . are waging a relentless struggle to erode the founding principles of the Turkish Republic, starting with secularism. . . . If necessary, the Turkish Armed Forces will not hesitate to make their position clear as the absolute defenders of secularism")—utterly fizzled, secular and religious Turks have spoken of a possible coup ever more abstractly. But if the army were to try, it is likely that very few senior officers, let alone the lesser ranks, as suggested by the *Ergenekon* indictments, in league with civilian officials and the Kemalist intelligentsia, would know anything about such plotting months in advance.

Dani Rodrik and Pinar Dogan, Harvard academics who are the son-in-law and daughter of retired four-star Gen. Çetin Dogan, who was arrested in the *Ergenekon* sweep, wrote a devastating critique of the whole affair in the *New Republic* magazine. They quote Gareth H. Jenkins, a British journalist-turned-Johns Hopkins scholar, who reviewed the voluminous indictments and came away with this conclusion: "the indictments are so full of contradictions, rumors, speculation, misinformation, illogicalities, absurdities, and untruths that they are not even internally consistent or coherent."

The Turkish military had been the firewall against ambitious Islamists, as it was a check on civilian secular governments that were seen to be weak and incompetent during times of civil strife. Turkish politics have always been rough. After the AKP won nearly 47 percent of the vote in the 2007 parliamentary elections—an impressive gain on its victorious 34 percent share in 2002—and after the party barely survived the effort by Aburrahman Yalçinkaya, the chief public prosecutor of the Supreme Court of Appeals and a staunch Kemalist, to bar the AKP and its leadership from politics, Erdogan has appeared ever more determined to get even with the military through the *Ergenekon* trials. Many Turks, especially on the left, where considerable bitterness remains from earlier coups against left-wing governments, like what Erdogan has done to the military even if some have been unsettled by his methods. Typical of this mindset is the commentary by Soli Ozel, a professor of international relations at Istanbul's Bilgi University and a columnist for the Turkish daily *Sabah*. Ozel, writing in a Brookings Institution study engagingly titled *Winning Turkey*, opines that with "the Constitutional Court's decision on the closure of the AKP and with the unfolding of the Ergenekon case, one can conclude that the days of military intervention and terror by rogue elements in Turkey are over. The political sphere now has an opportunity to build a truly civilian system where the rule of law is indeed supreme." But as Rodrik and Dogan point out, concern about the *Ergenekon* trial is not:

> . . . an argument for continued military domination of Turkish politics. Neither is it an argument for not going after the shadowy, clandestine networks with roots in the military that appear to have been involved in quite a few misdeeds. Kurdish sympathizers or suspected religious reactionaries have been treated harshly by the military and their civilian extensions, and have often been subject to dirty tricks themselves. But beyond the gross miscarriage of justice, the problem with today's judicial manipulation is that it makes it all the more difficult, if not impossible, for the real crimes to be uncovered and prosecuted. Once the deception is widely exposed, it is

not just the AKP government and the media that will take the hit. The judiciary will remain crippled for years, shorn of credibility. . . . This dirty war will come back to haunt them [Erdogan and his allies] once the Ergenekon and other trials unravel. The only beneficiaries will be the extremists, who will be ready to exploit the weakened state of the liberals and the moderate Islamists alike.

The *Ergenekon* case makes one fearfully wonder about the AKP's intentions. Prime Minister Erdogan certainly doesn't seem to want a more competitive, healthy political system, where faithful and secular Muslims vie for the country's soul (and political power and spoils) in free elections.

Fortunately Turkey's political system is no longer dependent on one man. Turkey is a large and increasingly diverse country, where economic, political, and religious power is becoming more fissiparous as it becomes more robust. All the deeply worrying trends under Justice and Development start to fade as one drives around Istanbul, through the miles of exurbs in Europe and Asia. Twenty-five years ago, I would have stopped that trip on the unpaved roads to the shantytowns—the *gecekondu* ("built in a night") shacks where poor, religious Turks from all over the country had come to find a better life. Such urban "villages" were ugly blemishes for Atatürk, who wanted all of Turkey to be like Pera, Istanbul's European quarter with its magnificent embassies to the Sublime Porte and white-gloved, fair-skinned women walking Independence Avenue, its main thoroughfare. He even held the peasant immigration to Istanbul at bay with troops at the railheads.

Today, many *gecekondus* have been transformed into and surrounded by massive middle-class and upper-middle-class communities. It took me two weeks in 2008 to weave my way through just a portion of the urban expansion on the European side of Istanbul; the growth on the Asian side has even been larger. Big religious neighborhoods with well-attended mosques abut teeming neighborhoods where far more people on Fridays drink at bars than pray. And the well-attended mosques were as I'd always found them in the Turkish countryside, open to foreigners and dialogue on just about any sensitive subject (which is not always the case in Istanbul, where some of the Ottoman Empire's great mosques have become militant and tense). Even in devoutly religious neighborhoods where the women were covered, I didn't have the impression that the AKP had a hold on the political loyalties of the faithful even though religious Turks told me that the secular parties didn't even bother to campaign regularly in their neighborhoods. The devout seemed little different than their secular brothers in their political commentary: they were deeply suspicious of the pecuniary habits of politicians who stayed too long in power. The AKP certainly has a big advantage with the poor. It is the only political party that has offices everywhere. The party of Atatürk, the Republican People's Party—better known by its Turkish initials CHP, the oldest political party in the country, the standard-bearer of the Kemalist center-left establishment—is rarely found in neighborhoods where no-alcohol "family" restaurants are the rule.

"The CHP are wine drinkers," a Turkish friend of mine said dismissively, revealing both his preference for the more masculine raki and why the CHP no longer tries to cultivate followers in religious neighborhoods. The CHP has become comfortable being the party of Bebek and Yeniköy, formerly quiet and trendy neighborhoods along the Bosporus that have exploded in size and wealth in the past ten years. The provocatively attired women in these neighborhoods rarely visit the old Istanbul within the walls of Constantinople, with all its congestion, veiled women, and large families picnicking in the parks along the Golden Horn and the Sea of Marmara.

But the CHP and the other secular political parties are not doomed to political marginality. All combined, they gathered as many votes as Justice and Development did in 2007. Understandably, Westerners always focus on the growth of religious identity among Muslims. It's real and it's easy to see. But there is also a reverse flow, where religious Muslims Westernize and secularize. I saw it in Marseille, a city I frequented in the 1990s, in its most religious quarters, where non-Muslim Frenchmen—*les Français de souche*—hardly ever entered. Among the first-generation youth it was unmistakable: more open manners, the way veiled women would unhesitatingly talk to foreigners, the way men and women used *je* and *moi*, "I" and "me," frequently and powerfully. This process, if hooked to a militant religious identity, can produce terrorist recruits; but here it produces Muslims who are mostly French. Militant Muslim bookstores in France and elsewhere in Europe usually have as many books about faithful Muslims being seduced by Western culture as they do Qur'anic commentaries and paeans to modern radical heroes such as Sayyid Qutb. Almost all of my *Français de souche* friends never saw this. They could see only the veils, the unshaven men, and the clogged streets where the male faithful would drop for prayers. I think the same phenomenon is happening in Turkey. The dominant Kemalist culture has been absorbing the faithful as much as the faithful have been absorbing Kemalism. The former is harder to see, especially for secular Turks who are more comfortable in Paris, London, and New York than they are in Konya, Erzurum, and Gaziantep. Atatürk, whose monumental tomb in Ankara is visited reverentially by legions of deeply religious Turks, was far more successful, and his cultural achievements far more secure, than many Turkish generals probably realize.

Graham Fuller isn't wrong when he writes that the Turkish public endured a "Kemalist historical lobotomy." The intrepid Turkish-speaking British journalist and author Hugh Pope is only pushing it a bit when he writes that the Turkish military "is an institution as ideologically trained and puritanical as the Islamic Revolutionary Guards in Iran." The Ottoman Empire was a wonderfully varied place, which could, at its best, be tolerant of differences in creed, tribe, and individual eccentricities. It would be good for the AKP, as well as the Kemalists, to be more multicultural. Neo-Ottomanism in this sense might just be what Turks need to become less fearful and more confident of their astonishing achievements.

It is obviously difficult to know where Erdogan and his AKP really want to take Turkey. But it's a decent bet that Turkey has Westernized so much that the AKP, even if one assumes the worst, will not be able to take the country back more steps than modern Turkish culture keeps pushing it forward. Turks are not blind: their diaspora has taken them everywhere, especially throughout the Middle East. They have seen the Iranian revolution and everything that has followed. They have seen Arab lands. They have seen Europe. They know that they are of two worlds, and they know which one has allowed Turkey to rise again as a great power. Unlike either the Arabs or the Iranians, they've been voting meaningfully for a few generations. Odds are that all hell would break loose, even among Turkey's most faithful, the moment the citizenry really thought the country had ceased being a democracy, or a stern society where proud Turkish men couldn't drink raki.

The Americans

WHAT SHOULD THE WEST—especially the United States—do as Islamists try to gain power in the Arab Middle East through the ballot box? (And they will definitely continue to try.) What should the Obama administration do vis-à-vis Iran and the Green Movement? What should it do vis-à-vis Turkey if the Justice and Development Party keeps indulging its autocratic ways? Many in the West just don't believe that Muslims can be democratic, at least not Arab and Iranian Muslims, who have had a poor track record of maintaining viable parliamentary systems. This school of thought emphasizes the West's slow, painful democratic evolution, the uniqueness of Occidental civilization, Islam's despotic history, and the modern cultural problems of Muslims (too tribal, too conspiratorial, too corrupt). The problems in Iraq, among the Palestinians, and farther afield in Afghanistan, have further fortified the pessimism about democracy's prospects in Muslim lands.

We now hear voices talking about reformulating American foreign policy toward the Middle East in terms of "exporting security," not democracy, or emphasizing, as President Obama does, "human dignity" and "mutual respect." It is not quite clear what Obama means. So far it seems a polite way of returning to a pre-9/11 world where Washington maintained tight military and intelligence relationships with many of the region's most oppressive regimes, generally said nice things about the rulers (we were concerned about their dignity), and didn't pry too deeply into any religious or cultural issues. If Arab Islamic democracies are never going to work, so this reasoning goes, and only lead to religious dictatorships, which will not help us with Bin Ladenism, let us just stick with the dictatorships that we have with all their familiar virtues and defects. In time, maybe the Muslims can work something out and finally become more like us. American liberalism appears to have lost its faith in liberty's ability to take root outside the West. So many American liberals, like the corporate Republicans of yesteryear, have developed a complacent acceptance of the "normalcy" of autocracy.

Let us first look at our fear of Arab Islamic democracies. Many Americans and Europeans would probably prefer to see secular dictatorships in power in the Arab Middle East that uphold modern Western standards on women's issues than see an Islamic democracy where the social and legal rights women enjoy in the West might be curtailed. They may well understand that dictatorships in the Middle East have done terrible things to their societies, including fertilizing the ground for Bin Ladenism, but they still cannot bring themselves to approve of a political process that could lead to the diminution of women's rights.

Others understandably look at minority rights for Christians and fear for their fate under Islamic democracies, where their numbers will be insufficient to guarantee them political power. Although many of them have increasingly flirted with Islamist causes and have been far from perfect in protecting Christians against bigoted Muslim irruptions, Middle Eastern secular dictatorships still maintain a certain protectorate over their Christian communities. Visits to Egypt's and Jordan's Red Sea resorts, where local Christians disproportionately come to relax and their women don Western clothing and manners, can quickly underscore why religious minorities are apprehensive of change in the political status quo.

As Islam democratizes, there surely will be a majoritarian problem in Arab states where Christians are present, because their numbers are too small to guarantee them an effective electoral means to block votes in parliament. (This might not be the case in Egypt with the Copts, who make up at least 10 percent of the population.) Factionalism will undoubtedly strike fundamentalist political parties, but this may not work to the advantage of Christians on sensitive issues such as public education, where Muslims may hold firm as a bloc. Since the birth of the secular Turkish republic, this majoritarian problem has caused Turkey's Christians, especially the Greeks and Armenians, considerable communal difficulty and individual indignities. In more overtly religious Muslim states where fundamentalists are politically predominant, Muslim consensus would likely work even more harshly against non-believers.

And then there is Israel, for whose well-being so many in America rightly fear. Some Muslim autocracies have signed peace treaties with Israel. They may not guarantee all that much, and certainly not the cultural reflection that ensures that the parties will not wage war again (think Germany and France). But the signed paper does exist. It is pretty hard to imagine any Arab Islamic democracy signing a peace treaty with Israel. For faithful Muslims, let alone fundamentalists, Israel is a Jewish-colonial-settler state, and all of Israel is Muslim land. What Hamas and the Egyptian Muslim Brotherhood say publicly is, in all probability, what Iraqi Prime Minister Nuri Kamal al-Maliki and Saudi King Abdullah say privately. The Fatah-Hamas imbroglio and the near certainty that another Hezbollah-like war between Israel and Hamas is in the future have just about shattered any democracy-for-Muslims enthusiasm that once existed in American circles that look at the Middle East through an Israeli security lens.

If we add up those who fear for Israel, Christians, and women, and those worried about intelligence and security relationships with Middle Eastern regimes, we find few American proponents of representative government in the Arab Middle East. The post-9/11 consensus on this issue, which was dominant among liberals, neoconservatives, and conservatives, has vanished.

But all of these concerns are shortsighted unless we really believe that Arab dictatorships over the past fifty years have evolved for the better. Hosni Mubarak is a less violent, more practical man than Nasser, but that difference does not give much comfort. On the street, Egyptian society seems to be falling apart, strained to its limits by demography and geography, but most importantly by a political regime that is incapable of responding to citizens' basic material needs and spiritual aspirations. Now, more than ever, Egyptians appear angry and humorless—an astonishing loss for what was once a good-humored and patient society. Mother Egypt, with its still-slick films and TV shows, has become the most effective exporter of anti-Semitism to the Arab world. A toxic mix of anti-Americanism, anti-Semitism, and antimodernism has overwhelmed Egyptian culture. The great modernists and skeptics in Egyptian letters and culture are all gone by now, or quite aged. Dictatorship has bred sterility, and little else.

Are Egyptian women's Western social rights really better protected in the long term by dictatorships, which have done a remarkably good job of turning more and more women, even among the elite attending the American University in Cairo, toward the veil and an embrace of "Islamic values"? If there is to be lasting social progress in Egypt and elsewhere in the Muslim Middle East, doesn't it require society as a whole, including both men and women, to embrace certain liberating ideas?

The notion that Westernized Muslim and Christian women in the Middle East can long sustain themselves in a secularism-hating sea of veils is delusional. What isn't delusional is the fact of Muslim evolution in the region. The Iranian revolution threw itself into "Islamic values"—some of which, like *chador*-clad women hoisting German assault-rifles on their shoulders, seem much more Western than Islamic. Yet only twenty years later, women said enough is enough. The Islamic republic, as we all know and fear it, would have fallen if women had been allowed to exercise their right to vote.

As long as women are allowed the right to vote—and no serious Muslim fundamentalist movement that has street power has advocated that women have less voting power than men (the Westernization of the Muslim mind is real)—the impact of the female vote on the future of Muslim societies will be profound and healthy. Muslim women may not vote the way Western women want them to, but they will surely vote in ways that increase their own security and the security of their children—and that cannot be bad. Decades ago the Princeton historian Bernard Lewis argued that the emancipation of women in the Muslim world was the key to the Middle East's peaceful and productive acceptance of modernity. Islam—and here it might be better to use the word the great Marshall Hodgson coined to convey the idea of the faith melding with a complex civilization, "Islamdom"—is a fraternity. I remember the exchange between a renowned professor of Islamic law and an inquiring female student, when she asked what happens to women when they go to heaven because the Qur'an does not allude to the rewards that devout women receive when they die. "Do they become *houris?*" the young lady asked. "Do they become men?" she continued. "It's not clear," the professor answered. "But I'm sure it's pleasant."

From the call to prayer, to the premodern chivalric associations that did so much to develop communal male character, to the veil that hides and restrains, as the medieval theologian Al-Ghazali tells us, insatiable female sexual power, to the sanctuary and privilege that every Muslim man can expect within his home, there is something deeply fraternal about Islam. It is not that Islamdom is a hypermasculine civilization; that inevitably follows in any society where violence is just below the surface. Islam is religiously, overwhelmingly a masculine voyage. And the empowerment of women is probably the only way to soften the faith's pride and curiosity. Women entering the workforce, which is occurring throughout the Middle East, is one way for that to happen. Also as important—and inextricably tied to economic progress—is the issue of women casting ballots. Evolution starts when Muslim men and women start voting; without elections, we will get more of what we have seen: more women and more men voting informally with their manners, clothes, prayers, and political associations against the dictatorial secularism that impoverishes their societies and makes them feel personally dirty.

The future of Israel is no different. Its security will be lasting only when Muslim peoples, not their ever-less popular governments, accept the Jewish homeland. This will probably take a long time. But evolution is the key, and the only way Muslim societies are going to evolve positively is through campaigns and elections. Hamas loathes Israel. But with elections, the Palestinian people may abandon the organization. Without competitive elections, which is essentially what we witnessed in Palestinian society from 1947 to Hamas's electoral victory, we saw political mores tailspin into the abyss. The cult of violence and of the gun wrecked Palestinian political culture. The same phenomenon has happened throughout the Middle East, but the situation is more severe among the Palestinians because they have been more intimately enmeshed in a losing *jihadist* psychology against the Israelis for sixty years.

Israel may soon have to fight a major war against Hamas. Regrettably, more wars with the Palestinian people may be down the road. But Israel will never have peace until Muslim Arabs, through their elected representatives, say enough is enough. What was true before World War II in Europe—where geographical, cultural, and religious animosities among the continent's many peoples were often savage—is surely true for Israelis and Muslim Arabs. Democracies eventually bring lasting peace. Dictatorships don't.

It is good to remember the observation made in 1986 by Professor Lewis in his seminal work *Semites and Anti-Semites*: "Muslim anti-Semitism is still something that comes from above, from the leadership, rather than from below, from the society." The average Arab or Iranian, who may be obsessed with Jewish conspiracies, is usually free of the personal contempt for Jews that marks the classical European or American anti-Semite. Democracy in the Muslim world would allow the best of the bottom (along with the worst) to rise to the top. This isn't going to eliminate Muslim anti-Semitism, which has risen under dictatorships and kings to truly frightening levels in the Middle East. Modern Islamic fundamentalism has turned a scorching spotlight back on the faith's foundation, when Jews, as the Qur'an tells us, stood in the way of the prophet and his divine mission. Ayatollah Khomeini's depiction of Jews in his masterpiece on Islamic government—"The Islamic movement was afflicted by the Jews from its very beginnings, when they began their hostile activity by distorting the reputation of Islam, and by defaming and maligning it. This has continued to the present day"—is the rule among Sunni and Shiite fundamentalists today. The Prophet Muhammad's slaughter of the Jewish Banu Qurayza tribe, which occasionally caused moral indigestion and apologia among classical and medieval Muslim commentators, serves as a leitmotif for contemporary radical Muslims, who often see Jews, as the Nazis once did, as innately and irreversibly evil. The tolerant, sometimes even philo-Semitic, attitudes of the Ottoman Empire have been nearly forgotten by Islam's modern militants (and Prime Minister Erdogan). And the Middle East's secular rulers, who often hobnob with visiting American and European Jews, have often mercilessly exploited anti-Semitism to strengthen their popular support (and in the case of the Mubarak regime, to deny that the peace treaty with Israel means all that much). Without the growth of a democratic culture in the Muslim world, it seems unlikely this disease can be countered and reversed.

Again an Iranian parallel is helpful. If Iranian voting actually counted, the war between the Islamic republic and Israel would have been over years ago. Many more Arab Muslims have detested Israel than has ever been the case in Iran, but at the time of the revolution anti-Zionism-as-anti-imperialism was popular among many, especially the well-educated pro-revolutionary youth. Anti-Semitism among Iran's prerevolutionary secular elite, let alone the Islamists, was rampant in the 1970s. This is certainly less true today. And to the extent that it isn't true, elections would have given real power to those who wanted to remove Iran from the anti-Israel *jihad*. It was common to see in the post–June 12, 2009, demonstrations young Iranians mocking the regime's embrace of the Palestinian cause with signs that read, "Palestine is not my country!"

If Iranian democracy were real, neither Israel nor the United States would be worrying much about a Persian nuke. The Iranians might well not build it given its enormous expense and the lack of any overpowering enemy on any front; and even if a democratic Iran chose to go nuclear, the fear of a transparent, democratic government in possession of nuclear weapons would not be so acute. Israel would not be staring at the horrific situation of Hezbollah in the north and Hamas in the south bombing its towns and cities with Iranian-supplied weaponry. A democratic Iran that had toppled its own Islamists would be unlikely to support the same people abroad. Democracy in Egypt might well shred the Israeli-Egyptian peace treaty, but if a democratic Egypt actually made a *de jure* agreement with the Jewish state, its ramifications on Muslim-Jewish relations would be profound, something not at all the case with the extremely cold peace between Jerusalem and Cairo today. The peace of a democratic society differs greatly from the peace secured by absolute monarchs and autocrats.

It will certainly be difficult for the United States to simultaneously support and criticize democracy in the Muslim world. When we cozy up to dictators, we are inclined to say nice things about them. When we engage other democracies, we want to esteem their values. Witness the Bush and Obama administrations' reluctance to criticize the Erdogan government in Ankara for harassing journalists, threatening free speech, and conducting outrageous show trials. This status quo disposition will, and should, be strained as Islamic democracy advances, because there will be severe points of friction between the United States and democratizing Islamic states (e.g., women, minority rights, homosexuality, Israel, Salman Rushdie–like affairs of free expression and inquiry). But we should take heart: Middle Eastern Muslims are largely playing on our field. Right and wrong in this globalized world is overwhelmingly defined by the West. This has been increasingly true ever since the British in 1807 outlawed the slave trade, an idea not welcomed by Muslims, who, like American Southerners, viewed slavery as vouchsafed to them by God. News of the decline of the West, and of America in particular, has been greatly exaggerated.

To give credit where credit is due: the ancient Greeks' inductive and deductive reasoning, which is so deep in our collective DNA, has given Westerners a huge material, rhetorical, and moral advantage. Anyone who has "engaged" revolutionary Iranians, face to face in open debate, knows this. The other side knows it, too. Which is why they, and the Saudis, usually try to hide or deny the worst things that they do (for example, stoning, beheading, or hanging women charged with moral crimes or slicing off the limbs of thieves). When Muslims demonstrated violently and nonviolently against the Danish cartoons lampooning the Prophet Muhammad, they were trying to partake in this globalized morals game. They were emulating us in our understanding of how cherished values know no borders. The Iranian parliament is a nonstop parade of cries and denunciations about what America has said or done. If you were to take away the West's commentary on the Muslim world and the Muslim reaction to it, many fundamentalist publishing houses would go out of business. For better or worse, in Muslims' minds we are the biggest bully pulpit.

As the idea of Islamic democracy grows in the Middle East, the West, especially the United States, will have an immense, healthy role—if we choose to take it—in providing "global" criticism of what Muslims are doing. For all concerned, but especially for our own well-being, we should be fully engaged in the great ethical and political debates that are developing in the Middle East, debates which 9/11 and its aftermath have kicked into high gear. With or without us, Muslims in the Middle East are moving in a democratic direction. Their basic understanding of who they are as a community of faithful men and women propels them. We don't know whether their experiment with representative government will succeed or fail. Majoritarian democracy, which is what we are likely to see at least in the early years of fundamentalist-dominated governments in the Arab world, can always crack in wild swings of passion and suspicion. They will have to confront by trial and error the majority and minority concerns that James Madison so ingeniously tackled in the Constitution.

But surely devout Muslims should have the right to try. They have come an enormous distance since the Prophet Muhammad first heard God's call. A basic respect for the dignity of Muslims as believers and citizens of the states they live in ought to incline the West not to praise and indulge the Middle East's ruling elites, who have shown little regard for the people below them. The Second Iraq War may have exhausted the patience and tested the optimism of most Americans and turned liberal internationalists into die-hard "realists" and conservatives into isolationists. But we, of all people, should know you can't stop evolution. The events of 9/11 should have irrevocably taught us that we want more of it, not less. Middle Eastern autocrats offer only an illusion of progress and security. Since World War II, they have, with only a few exceptions, impoverished their societies.

And with Iran, finding the right policy shouldn't be that difficult. The Green Movement is, after all, what several American administrations have dreamed of since 1979. As with the Soviet Union, the Islamic republic's internal contradictions have finally taken their toll. American policy should obviously aim to fortify those forces that produced the Green Movement, which is the most powerful collection of liberal democrats ever in the Muslim Middle East. The Iranian and Arab paths to democracy will likely be very different, but Iranians could lead the way to a more liberal order (as could the Turks, too). We should want them to try. Instead of declaring that "I consider it part of my responsibility as president of the United States to fight against negative stereotypes of Islam wherever they appear" and suggesting that he personally knows "what Islam is" and "what it isn't," President Obama could, perhaps, let Muslims decide the content of their faith and handle whatever negative stereotyping has been done by nefarious Westerners. The Green Movement screams out one truth: we are adults! We, as Muslims, are capable of governing ourselves. We can delve into our faith and culture and expose the ugliness—Khatami's "pathology of despotism"—within. From 1979 to 2009, the United States had the consistent position that there was something morally and inexcusably amiss with the Islamic revolution. Iranians have been saying the same thing much more trenchantly. It is not in the United States' interest to go easy on Islam and the Middle East's autocracies. We should respectfully but unflinchingly ask tough questions, especially as democratic movements appear in the region. When we do, as Iran's democratic intellectual revolution has shown, Muslims invariably answer. We deserve a little credit—the Iranians deserve far more—for keeping the spotlight on tyranny. Iranians certainly deserve the same kind of moral and practical support today that the Reagan administration gave the Poles under communism. The Poles broke communism; if the Iranians can establish a democracy, they could shatter the secular and religious authoritarianism that has made the Middle East the most embittered and angriest place on earth.

The promise of democracy for Muslims offers something historically unparalleled. For the first time since the early caliphs, it holds out the possibility that there will be an organic, reciprocal relationship between leaders and their communities. It could end Islam's long history of rebellious violence and redirect the faith's unrequited quest for more virtuous men. It could give the Middle East's Muslims some of the elemental, nonthreatening, unflappable pride and self-confidence that Americans, the oldest modern democrats, have in spades. In an age of proliferating nuclear weapons, that would be a very good thing for believers and nonbelievers alike.

AFTERWORD

THE WAVE HAS ARRIVED. What started in Tunisia and then spread to Egypt—the two oldest modern Arab states—has now engulfed the region, dethroning two of the most "secure" dictators and scaring every other "president," amir, and king. Inspired (and undoubtedly shamed) by the Great Arab Revolt to the west, the Green Movement in Iran has been reborn, provoking the regime to arrest two of its leaders, Mehdi Karroubi and Mir Hussein Moussavi, men widely respected within what is left of the ruling establishment. This move, especially if it is followed by their trial, may prove a turning point. Iran's supreme ruler has tried to squash the Green Movement through executions, imprisonment, torture, and exile; it has not worked. Ali Khameneh'i is now running the risk of making martyrs of two revolutionaries who at one time carried more of the mantle of Ruhollah Khomeini than he did.

If the Arab rebellion had not happened, Khameneh'i might have lucked out: through brutal repression, he might have silenced the pro-democracy forces for a few more years. But a democratic dynamic has developed in the Middle East, where what happens in one country feeds aspirations elsewhere. Iran and Egypt, the only Arab country the Persians have ever taken seriously, are likely wedded to each other now: if one goes democratic, the centripetal effect will probably convert the other. The great historic divides in the region—between Arabs and Iranians, Sunnis and Shiites—matter less as universal ideas gain ground throughout the region. These ideas are preeminently one man-one vote and the West's most pernicious and contagious idea, individualism, which wreaks as much havoc among traditional religious societies as it does within Marxist states. (Democracy does, of course, scare Sunni Arabs in states like Bahrain and Iraq, where they have lorded it over much more numerous Shiites.)

Jurat—courage—is a tricky attribute in the Muslim Middle East. The ruling upper classes have always feared its ignition among intellectuals and the poor even though they've usually treated the citizenry as sheep. As a case officer, I was regularly astounded to see timid Arab and Iranian men, in whom obsequiousness was second nature, use association with the CIA—the act of espionage—as a vehicle for individual empowerment and revenge. And once *jurat* was unleashed in them, it didn't relent, even under the most harrowing circumstances. In the Middle East today, the oppressed can see a chance for victory. Anger at injustice is the common denominator of all Muslim societies from Morocco to Iran. The remaining autocrats of the region, the security establishments behind them, and just about everyone in Israel are surely hoping that the wave ebbs and that the Middle East in a year looks, more or less, like the Middle East before Zine al-Abidine Ben Ali and Hosni Mubarak fell. But Tunisian Mohamed Bouazizi's self-immolation started something that is unlikely to abate. Most probably, 2011, like 1979, is irreversibly transformative. In five years, for better or worse (the odds are with the former, not the latter), the Middle East as we have known it will likely be unrecognizable.

It is still striking, three months into the Great Arab Revolt, how timorously many Westerners greet the region-wide uprising. Recognizing that democratic aspirations may be only a small factor in all the tumult, many would prefer to focus on the particulars of the revolts—the Shiite-Sunni split in Bahrain, the Palestinian-Jordanian tension in the Hashemite Kingdom, the outrageous corruption in Tunisia, the tribal jealousies and Orwellian bizarreness of Muammar Qaddafi's Libya, the haughty (and in private deviant) autocracy in Morocco, the too-duplicitous dictatorship of Yemeni president Ali Abdullah Saleh, who rides shotgun over a deep Sunni-Shiite tribal divide, and the desiccated authoritarianism of Mubarak.

And even though Islam has hardly raised its head in all of these disturbances—*Allahu Akbar!* is most often uttered as a fraternal, please-don't-shoot appeal from young men and women to soldiers and not as a war cry—the West's unease with all of these revolts is clearly traceable to the fear that religion will cause Muslims freed of their dictators to run amok. Seeing Western parallels with the wave of revolutions that swept Europe in 1848—rather than with the more successful, more cleanly ideological, and thus more noble rebellions against communism in 1989—these commentators express, at best, a hopeful diffidence about what is transpiring. After all, we expect reactionaries to triumph in the Muslim Middle East—haven't they always?—and we can't really embrace the opposition because so much of it is culturally unpleasant and unpredictable.

Thus Americans and Britons, who've always supplied proficient security advisors to the Bahraini royal family, are comfortable with Manama's Sunni elite, which is highly Western-ized—quite capable, for instance, of hosting private pool parties where Sunni Bahraini women chat with Western men. Shiite Bahraini women, who've been bravely taking to the streets, are mostly dressed in black *chadors*. In any sizing up of the situation—with the U.S. Fifth Fleet anchored in Bahrain and the *chador*-wearing Iranians across the Gulf—these things matter. The Muslim Middle East hasn't produced Václav Havels and Nelson Mandelas—resolutely democratic intellectuals of stature and moral bearing who've suffered se-verely but risen above vengeance to inspire a belief that this will all work out. (Egypt's Saad Eddin Ibrahim is as close as we get.) Members of the Middle East's Facebook generation, impressive as they've been in protest and notably free of the utopianism that plagued their pan-Arabist, Arab nationalist, and Islamist grandfathers and fathers, are, nonetheless, by def-inition leaderless and, like all young men and women, still mostly unmolded clay.

But these commentators, often thoughtful and not mean-spirited toward Muslims, are reading the dynamics in reverse. It's the universals—especially the democratic ideals—that have welded together the particular complaints into revolt. This democratic sentiment isn't often sophisticated and lib-erally expressed, but it is deeply felt in the most basic and important way: Arabs and Iranians want to vote for their leaders. Elections for them, as for us, are the sine qua non of a legitimate political order. In Egypt, now as always the bell-wether for Arab lands, the liberal, nationalist tradition is in the process of remaking itself. Corrupt and comatose under Mubarak, the Wafd Party will come back, as will surely the Liberal Constitutionalist tradition that once offered such promise when British traditions still had magnetic power.

(The Ghad Party of Ayman Nour is an echo of this once great force.)

It is extremely important to note that nowhere in the rebellious lands have we heard Muslim fundamentalists openly challenging the notion that elections are the moral imperative of our time. In Egypt, we've already seen younger members of the Muslim Brotherhood, who were the driving force behind the aborted 2007 platform, openly affirm their faith in democracy and question the commitment of their elders to representative government. Thirty years ago in Iran, there was never any deception on the part of Ayatollah Khomeini about what he intended to do. The *New York Times* may have thought that Khomeini was an "enigma," Senator Edward Kennedy may have seen a turbaned George Washington, but that misreading was not due to clever obfuscation by wily, deceiving mullahs. As the historian Bernard Lewis tried to inform the State Department in 1979, the ayatollah's writings were crystal clear: he intended to establish a theocracy. (And even then, a theocracy with "elections.")

The Egyptian Muslim Brotherhood, an organization born and raised in clandestine opposition to foreign occupation and domestic dictatorship, has many profound misgivings about democracy. There's not a fundamentalist alive who doesn't have misgivings. But what is extraordinary to note about the Brotherhood, since the rebellion in Tunisia began, is the extent to which it has publicly and passionately embraced the idea that democracy is the only legitimate political system for Egypt and the rest of the Muslim world.

The current leader of the Brotherhood, Mohammed Badie, like his predecessor, the always frightful Muhammad Mahdi Akef, may well dream of a reborn caliphate—Sunni fundamentalists have been romantically attached to this idea since Atatürk abolished the Ottoman caliphate in 1924—but the notion has no political relevance in Egypt today, and the Muslim Brotherhood knows it. Islamist organizations have played a small role in the uprisings throughout the Middle East because they, more than anyone else, know their world is in rapid transition.

Islamists are bottom feeders: they know what's going on among the urban poor. In 1990, Ali Belhadj, the fiery anti-democratic powerhouse of the Islamic Salvation Front in Algeria, could plausibly hope to rally enough Algerians to his authoritarian Islamist banner. In 2011, after the palpable failure of the Islamic revolution in Iran, after twenty years of the democratization of Egypt's intellectual life, which obliged the Muslim Brotherhood to wrestle openly with the democratic ethos in ways that it never had before, Islamic fundamentalists do not view themselves as having the upper hand, and in Egypt have been downright honest in confessing that the Great Arab Revolt isn't theirs. (Khomeini, by comparison, claimed credit for everything.) In Tunisia, Egypt, Jordan, and perhaps even in Algeria, where the memories of the civil war appear to have dulled the emotions and expectations of the pro-democracy demonstrators, Islamists certainly remain hopeful.

And they will, no doubt, rally. The secular dictatorships, which Western powers once thought so progressive, have warped national identities throughout the region. (This is much less true in Egypt and Tunisia, where the modern national identity is older and more solid than elsewhere in the Arab world.) In this desolation, the Islamic identity—the root identity of the Middle East—has grown stronger.

But Islamism is trying hard to make the jump into the democratic age, which is now arriving in force. Islamists today sincerely hope that most Muslims will be good Muslims (as I've discussed earlier, the Sunni Islamic tradition doesn't really recognize the philosophical possibility that a majority of the faithful could be bad Muslims), and therefore they affirm the democratic promise. But they know they are going into uncharted territory. Many in the West fear an Islamist wave that democracy could bring; Islamists fear that Western fears are unfounded.

We should still worry about the power of Saudi Arabia and its Wahhabi missionary machine. The desert kingdom may "luck out" and miss the democratic wave. Among the least Westernized of oil states, where the monarchy is intertwined with the Wahhabi religious establishment, democratic pressure may not build from either the secular left or the religious right—the pincer movement that will likely doom dictatorial rule throughout North Africa and the Near East. We are not accustomed to seeing Saudi Arabia as a backwater of the Islamic world—its oil wealth and the hajj pilgrimage have given it unparalleled prominence. But the new age in the Middle East could be very unkind to the Saudis. Despite the wealth behind it, Saudi Arabia's Wahhabi ideology, which has done so much damage to Islamic diversity and which helped to birth Osama bin Laden, is already running into a powerful democratic ethos outside of Arabia. Muslim historians have always looked at the hajj as a huge intellectual pump pushing ideas everywhere in Islamic civilization. The Saudis have energetically used the hajj to pump their ideas into the Muslim bloodstream. But it's a two-way flow. We will soon likely see how insular and unique Saudi Arabia really is. It's not inconceivable that Westernized Saudis and pro-democracy Islamic dissidents could shake the Saudis' comfortable marriage with the virulently anti-democratic Wahhabi establishment.

As I've underscored throughout this book, there is no guarantee that Arab democracies, assuming they are born, will be particularly friendly to the United States. What we are likely to see in the Middle East is a variant of what we have seen in a democratizing Latin America, which like the Muslim Middle East had a tense history with the United States in the twentieth century. Democratically empowered Latin Americans, now and then, like to stick it to Americans. (And only a historically purblind American patriot would deny them that pleasure.) But as democratically empowered Latin Americans have become rapidly more responsible at home, they have become less emotional, less prideful—descriptions we often hear applied to the denizens of the Middle East—in their dealings with Americans. Latin American democratic experiments can go awry; they have in Venezuela and Nicaragua. But in neither case is the situation hopeless, precisely because the democratic ethos—however badly mauled—lives on in these countries. The Venezuelan people remain our best bet for getting rid of Hugo Chávez.

Democracy in the Middle East will likely be rougher for the United States. Long-held conspiracy theories and animosities against the "imperial" West—especially "Zionist-controlled America"—live on in left-wing Arab and Iranian intellectual circles, which will probably get a new lease on life with the coming of democracy. More fundamentally, the Middle East is a Muslim region whose medieval and modern identities were in great part formed in opposition to Christendom and the West. The most elemental reflexes are infelicitous.

But working against this history is the idea of America—a revolutionary bastion of the democratic common man where all have a chance for happiness—that still finds its way into the bloodstream of the Muslim Middle East. This is an abstract notion, often far less noticeable than the traditional animosity bred by Islam and the Islamist animosity bred by modernity's (that is, America's) unrelenting advance. But it is powerful nonetheless, which is why Egyptian protesters could be heard to complain vociferously about America's diffidence in supporting their cause. The anger at Europeans was less because far less is expected of them.

The Obama administration is obviously having a hard time with the Great Arab Revolt. In Egypt, President Obama finally saved the ship of state from a "realist" wreck by making it clear that he sided with the demonstrators and not the regime of Hosni Mubarak. But the president is still off balance in the Middle East, a region he does not know. As *The New Republic*'s Leon Wielsetier has observed, Mr. Obama dreads the United States being labeled an "imperialist" power. The president's youthful *tier-mondiste* sentiments are still with him.

The inexcusable wobbling—when firm condemnation of the bloodlust of Libya's savage ruler was called for—suggests that the president's non-interventionist, anti-imperialist roots, which meld almost indistinguishably into the "realist" tradition of George H.W. Bush, for which President Obama has great respect, are still stronger than his sincere concern for third-worlders struggling for freedom.

The administration may well play an inconsistent game, trying to support democracy seriously in Egypt, which is the all-critical Arab state, but less seriously elsewhere. This will be a mistake, inviting the contempt of Arabs and the possible collapse of U.S. democracy promotion everywhere. The Khalifa family in Bahrain and the Hashemite monarchy in Jordan should be under no illusions about where America's heart and wallet are. Americans should always be in favor of orderly change, which is why the Khalifas and Hashemites should start now to transfer political power gradually to the Shia in Bahrain and the Palestinians in Jordan. They may possibly save their monarchies by doing so (and save us a fairly good friend on the East Bank of the Jordan River and the anchorage of the Fifth Fleet in the Persian Gulf). No one should want to see the Israelis, who understandably fear a new Middle East where nothing is secure and the Muslim Brotherhood gets to vie for votes, traumatized. Americans really don't want to see the Saudi armed forces rolling across the Gulf causeway to crush democratic protests in Bahrain. If we wanted to create a situation that Iran could exploit, that would be it. If we wanted to ignite sectarian strife throughout the region, that would be how to do it.

The United States has an enormous role to play midwifing democracy throughout the Middle East. And President Obama, if he could realize this despite his profound unease at becoming the successor to the freedom-promoting George W. Bush, might go down in history as America's great third-world president—the man who permanently buried our dependency on Arab despots. When I closed this book in October of 2010 with the suggestion that democratic convulsions in the Middle East could likely become the defining theme of Barack Obama's presidency, it seemed a bold, if not downright addle-headed, prediction. This will now undoubtedly be Mr. Obama's fate. It's too soon to know how the president will rise to the challenge. But one thing is certain: the age of "Islamic exceptionalism" is over. At full speed, the

Middle East is engaging the modern democratic era. It will probably be one hell of a ride. Reaction here and there may get the better of the cause and turn some countries into bloody messes. But both God and man are now behind the democratic promise. Nothing is inevitable, but that is a very hard combination to stop.

BIBLIOGRAPHY

Fariba Abdelkhah, *Being Modern in Iran* (New York: Columbia University Press, 2000)

Geneive Abdo, *No God but God: Egypt and the Triumph of Islam* (New York: Oxford University Press, 2000)

Khaled Abou El Fadl, *The Authoritative and the Authoritarian in Islamic Discourses* (Alexandria, VA: Al-Saadawi Publications, 2002)

John Agresto, *Mugged by Reality: The Liberation of Iraq and the Failure of Good Intentions* (New York: Encounter Books, 2007)

M. al-Ahnaf, Bernard Botiveau, and Franck Frégosi, *L'Algerie par ses Islamistes* (Paris: Karthala, 1991)

Fouad Ajami, *The Arab Predicament* (Cambridge: Cambridge University Press, 1981)

———, *The Dream Palace of the Arabs: A Generation's Odyssey* (New York: Pantheon Books, 1998)

Ali A. Allawi, *The Crisis of Islamic Civilization* (New Haven and London: Yale University Press, 2009)

The Al-Qaeda Reader, ed. and trans. Raymond Ibrahim (New York: Doubleday, 2007)

Peter Beinart, "A Different Country," *New Republic*, March 5, 2007, and "Tony Award," *New Republic*, July 3, 2006

Jonathan P. Berkey, *The Formation of Islam: Religion and Society in the Near East, 600–1800* (New York: Cambridge University Press, 2005)

Richard Bulliet, "The Crisis of Authority in Islam," *Wilson Quarterly*, Winter 2002, Vol. 26

François Burgat and William Dowell, *The Islamic Movement in North Africa* (Austin: Center for Middle Eastern Studies at the University of Texas, Middle East Monograph Series, 1993)

E. Chehabi, *Iranian Politics and Religious Modernism* (Ithaca and New York: Cornell University Press, 1990)

David Commins, *The Wahhabi Mission and Saudi Arabia* (London and New York: I.B. Tauris, 2009)

Michael Cook, *Commanding Right and Forbidding Wrong in Islamic Thought* (New York and Cambridge: Cambridge University Press, 2002)

N.J. Coulson, *A History of Islamic Law* (Edinburgh: Edinburgh University Press, 1971)

Patricia Crone, *God's Rule—Government and Islam: Six Centuries of Medieval Islamic Political Thought* (New York: Columbia University Press, 2004)

Patricia Crone and Martin Hinds, *God's Caliph: Religious Authority in the First Centuries of Islam* (Cambridge: Cambridge University Press, 2003)

Adeed Dawisha, *The Arab Radicals* (New York: The Council on Foreign Relations, 1986)

Maureen Dowd, *Meet the Press*, NBC, September 25, 2005

Martin Evans and John Phillips, *Algeria: Anger of the Dispossessed* (New Haven and London: Yale University Press, 2007)

Charles Freeman, *The Closing of the Western Mind: The Rise of Faith and the Fall of Reason* (New York: Vintage Books, 2005)

Graham E. Fuller, *The New Turkish Republic: Turkey as a Pivitol State in the Muslim World* (Washington, DC: United States Institute of Peace Press, 2008)

Akbar Ganji, *The Road to Democracy in Iran* (Cambridge, Mass: MIT Press, 2008)

Reuel Marc Gerecht, *The Islamic Paradox: Shiite Clerics, Sunni Fundamentalists, and the Coming of Arab Democracy* (Washington, DC: AEI Press, 2004)

————, "Iran: Fundamentalism and Reform," in *Present Dangers*, eds. Robert Kagan and William Kristol (New York: Encounter Books, 2000)

Philip Gordon and Omer Taspinar, *Winning Turkey: How America, Europe, and Turkey Can Revive a Fading Partnership* (Washington, DC: Brookings Institution, 2008)

Patrick Haenni, "Ils n'en ont pas fini avec l'Orient: de quelques islamisations non islamistes," *Le post-islamisme*, eds. Olivier Roy and Patrick Haenni (Aix-en-Provence: Éditions ÉDISUD, 1999)

Marshall Hodgson, *The Venture of Islam*, vol. 1, *The Classical Age of Islam* (Chicago: Chicago University Press, 1974) and *The Venture of Islam*, vol. 2, *The Expansion of Islam in the Middle Periods* (Chicago: Chicago University Press, 1974)

Bernard Hourcade and Yann Richard, *Téhéran Au Dessous du Volcan* (Paris: Autrement, 1987)

Samuel P. Huntington, *The Third Wave: Democratization in the Late Twentieth Century* (Norman: University of Oklahoma Press, 1991)

Charles Issawi, *The Arab World's Legacy* (Princeton: The Darwin Press, 1981)

Gary Kamiya, "The Road to Hell," *Salon.com*, October 7, 2005, http://dir.salon.com/story/books/review/2005/10/07/packer/index.html

Mehran Kamrava, *Iran's Intellectual Revolution* (Cambridge: Cambridge University Press, 2008)

Michael Kelly, *Martyrs' Day: Chronicles of a Small War* (New York: Random House, 1993) and his *Washington Post* articles: "Who Would Choose Tyranny?" *Washington Post*, February 26, 2003; "Immorality on the March," *Washington Post*, February 19, 2003; and "Marching with Stalinists," *Washington Post*, January 22, 2003

Gilles Kepel and Yann Richard, eds., *Intellectuels et militants de l'Islam contemporain* (Paris: Seuil, 1990)

Mohammad Khatami, *Az donya-ye shahr ta shahr-e donya: sayri dar andisheh-ye siyasi-e gharb* [From the world city to the city world: a voyage through the political thought of the West] (Tehran: Nashrani 1376/1997) and *Bim-e mawj* [Fear of the wave] (Tehran: Sima-ye javan, 1373/1994)

Farhad Khosrokhavar and Olivier Roy, *Iran: Comment sortir d'une révolution religieuse* (Paris: Éditions du Seuil, 1999)

Farhad Khosrokhavar, *Avoir vingt ans au pays des ayatollahs: vivre dans la ville sainte de Qom* (Paris: Robert Laffont, 2009)

———, *l'Utopie Sacrifiée: Sociologie de la révolution iranienne* (Paris: Presses de la Fondation Nationale des Sciences Politiques, 1993)

Bernard Lewis, *Islam and the West* (New York and Oxford: Oxford University Press, 1993)

————, *Semites and Anti-Semites* (New York: W.W. Norton, 1986)

————, *The Multiple Identities of the Middle East* (New York: Schocken Books, 1998)

————, *The Muslim Discovery of Europe* (New York and London: Norton, 2001)

Geoffrey Lewis, *Modern Turkey* (New York and Washington: Praeger Publishers, 1974)

Mark Lynch, "The Brotherhood's Dilemma," Middle East Brief of the Crown Center for Middle East Studies, number 25, Brandeis University, January 2008

————, "Islamist Views of Reform," paper presented at the Brookings Institution's U.S.-Islamic World Forum, Doha, Qatar, February 16–18, 2008

Al-Masry Al-Youm, August 10–14, 2007. See http://www.almasry-alyoum.com/article2.aspx?ArticleID 1826. The second installment, on August 11, is about economic development, development policies, and the service/commodity sectors; see http://www.almasry-alyoum.com/article2.aspx?ArticleID 1861. The third installment, on August 12, is about national security, foreign policy, and Egyptian society; see http://www.almasry-alyoum.com/article2.aspx?ArticleID 2042. The fourth installment, on August 14, is about culture, women, youth, sports, the arts, and the media; see http://www.almasry-alyoum.com/article2.aspx?ArticleID 2215

Richard P. Mitchell, *The Society of the Muslim Brothers* (New York and Oxford: Oxford University Press, 1993)

Mansoor Moaddel and Kamran Talattof, eds., *Modernist and Fundamentalist Debates in Islam* (New York: Palgrave Macmillian, 2000)

Modernist Islam, 1840–1940: A Sourcebook, ed. Charles Kurzman (New York: Oxford University Press, 2002)

Mohammad Mojtahed-Shabestari, *Iman va Azadi* [Faith and Freedom](Tehran: Tarh-e No, 1379/2000)

Momayyezi Ketab: Pazuheshi dar hazar o chahar sad sanad-e momayyezi ketab [Censorship: A review of 1,400 documents from the Office of Book Censorship] (Tehran: Entesharat-e Kavir, 1380/2001)

Vali Nasr, *Forces of Fortune* (New York: Free Press, 2009)

Abdallah Nouri, *Shokaran-e Eslah: Defa'iyyat-e Abdallah Nuri* [The Hemlock of reform: The defense of Abdallah Nouri] (Tehran: Tarh-e No, 1378/1999)

George Packer, *The Assassins' Gate* (New York: Farrar, Straus, and Giroux, 2005)

Jaroslav Pelikan, *Jesus Through the Centuries: His Place in the History of Culture* (New Haven and London: Yale University Press, 1985)

David Pollack, "Slippery Polls: Uses and Abuses of Opinion Surveys from Arab States," Washington Institute for Near East Policy, Policy Focus #82, April 2008

Nicole Pope and Hugh Pope, *Turkey Unveiled: A History of Modern Turkey* (Woodstock and New York: The Overlook Press, 1997/2004)

Fazlur Rahman, *Islam and Modernity* (Chicago and London: University of Chicago Press, 1982)

Donald Malcolm Reid, *Cairo University and the making of modern Egypt* (Cambridge: Cambridge University Press, 1990)

Maxime Rodinson, *L'Islam: Politique et croyance* (Paris: Fayard, 1993)

Ahmad Rouadjia, *Les frères et la mosquée: Enquête sur le mouvement islamiste en Algérie* (Paris: Karthala, 1990)

Olivier Roy, *Généalogie de l'islamisme* (Paris: Hachette Littér-
     atures, 2001)

————, *Secularism Confronts Islam*, uncorrected proof (New
     York: Columbia University Press, 2007)

Ali Shariati, *Ali* (Tehran: Intesharat-e Nilufer, 1983)

Emmanuel Sivan, *Radical Islam, Medieval Theology and Mod-
     ern Politics* (New Haven and London: Yale University
     Press, 1985)

Abdolkarim Soroush, *Reason, Freedom, and Democracy in Is-
     lam*, eds. Mahmoud Sadri and Ahmad Sadri (Oxford: Ox-
     ford University Press, 2000)

Alexis de Tocqueville, *Democracy in America* (New York: Al-
     fred A. Knopf, 1980)

Paul Vieille and Farhad Khosrokhavar, *Le Discours populaire
     de la révolution iranienne*, vols. 1 and 2 (Paris: Contem-
     poranéité, 1990)

William Montgomery Watt, *Islamic Philosophy and Theology*
     (Edinburgh: Edinburgh University Press, 1962)

————, *Muhammad at Mecca* (Oxford: Oxford University
     Press, 1953)

————, *Muhammad at Medina* (Oxford: Oxford University
     Press, 1956)

Max Weber, *Economy and Society*, eds. Guenther Roth and
     Claus Wittich (Berkeley and London: University of Cal-
     ifornia Press, 1978)

Malika Zeghlal, *Gardiens de L'Islam. Les oulemas d'Al-Azhar
     dan l'Egypte contemporaine* (Paris: Presse de Sciences Po,
     1996)

RECOMMENDED READING

Literature on democracy and Islam has generally come in two different categories: scholarly and exuberantly rose-colored or journalistic and pretty depressing. Oddly, the scholarly writing on the subject has often been ahistorical, giving little attention to the centuries when Islam developed under the caliphs and sultans. I think this is done for two reasons: modernists don't like going medieval (as medievalists often shun modern times), and any serious historical discussion of Islamic thought, for a scholar who wants to see democratic possibilities in the faith, is depressing. But it doesn't need to be *that* depressing.

My reading list, which lies behind this book, is eclectic: I think you have to come at modern Islamic history early, and you need to come at it from several different angles. Accordingly, I can't really recommend, except when dealing with the intellectual rise of the Green Movement in Iran, just a few books that will allow the reader to build rapidly on (or completely deconstruct) what I've written.

But here is my list. On Islamic history, it's really impossible to go anywhere without reading Bernard Lewis's *The Muslim Discovery of Europe*. It is the foundation for all discussions about East meets West. Also see Professor Lewis's

Islam and the West, which contains a must-read essay on "Religious Coexistence and Secularism." Also essential is Patricia Crone's *God's Rule—Government and Islam: Six Centuries of Medieval Islamic Political Thought*, as is her and Martin Hinds's *God's Caliph: Religious Authority in the First Centuries of Islam*. Michael Cook's magisterial *Commanding Right and Forbidding Wrong in Islamic Thought* is also obligatory. Islamic militants, like traditionalists, are never far from thinking about the Qu'ranic injunction to command right and forbid wrong. Cook's history of Islam's "categorical imperative" is unrivaled. Jonathan P. Berkey's *The Formation of Islam: Religion and Society in the Near East, 600–1800* is also a wonderful work for seeing both the broad brushstrokes and small corners of Islam's religious-political fusion. Having a basic understanding of Islamic law also is a must, and N.J. Coulson's short but compendious *A History of Islamic Law* does the trick. W. Montgomery Watt's *Islamic Philosophy and Theology* is also an invaluable book for the general reader. Although it was written nearly fifty years ago, its insights are as good now as they were then. And last but not least, it's a good idea to read the great French scholar Maxime Rodinson's *L'Islam: Politique et croyance*. Rodinson boils down decades of his ruminations on the Islamic world. Because Rodinson was a Marxist, he provides, at times, an interesting angle, one less common in English, that can be helpful since many of the great Muslim minds of the modern era were educated in France or in French, often with a Marxist twist.

On the Arabs, Fouad Ajami's *The Arab Predicament* is perhaps the best one-volume treatment on contemporary Arab thought and history. The problems of political and cultural legitimacy are at the heart of this book and at the core of any political evolution we will see in the future in the Arab world. Professor Ajami's more literary sequel, *The Dream Palace of the Arabs*, revisits the same themes, showing the reader, perhaps better than any other book in English, how poorly— tragically—Arab intellectuals have handled modernity. In the same vein, the essays of the late Charles Issawi in *The Arab World's Legacy* are a must-read. The book does not do justice to Professor Issawi's always affectionate and wry ability to dissect the Arab world's "heavy legacy," but it is, nonetheless, a sufficiently depressing read. Emmanuel Sivan's *Radical Islam* is essential for an understanding of militant Islam's evolution, especially among the Arabs. Adeed Dawisha's *The Arab Radicals* is also helpful with the same terrain. Noah Feldman's *After Jihad: America and the Struggle for Islamic Democracy* is a worthwhile read since Professor Feldman worked with Iraqis after the fall of Saddam and his background in Islamic law always keeps the reader cognizant of the historical obstacles to democracy's growth in the Middle East. Geneive Abdo's *No God but God: Egypt and the Triumph of Islam* is probably the best book about Egypt's political-religious travails and opportunities. And François Burgat's and William Dowell's *The Islamic Movement in North Africa* is good for understanding the genesis of Islamic activism in the Arab West.

On the Iranians, we are blessed with riches. By far the best treatment of Iran's "second intellectual revolution" is Mehran Kamrava's *Iran's Intellectual Revolution*. Professor Kamrava does a sublimely good job of simplifying the complexity of Iran's evolving religious and secular political thought, and I have drawn from his work extensively here. For understanding the evolution of what has become the Green Movement, there is no more important book. Farhad Khosrokhavar's and Olivier Roy's *Iran: Comment sortir d'une révolution religieuse* is also good for understanding the intellectual yeast behind Iran's pro-democracy movement and the increasing secularization of Iranian society under religious rule. Khosrokhavar's *Avoir vingt ans au pays des ayatollahs* is also an important work for understanding how profoundly Westernization has seized Iranians, even in the clerical city of Qom. And the writings of Abdolkarim Soroush in his *Reason, Freedom, and Democracy in Islam* should not be missed. Soroush's subject is much larger than Iran, but his essays on the Islamic world in this work can give the reader some idea of how religiously progressive Soroush is and why he became a cult figure on Iranian campuses fifteen years ago.

On the Turks, Bernard Lewis's *The Emergence of Modern Turkey* remains key in understanding the evolution of Kemalism. I also like Nicole Pope's and Hugh Pope's *Turkey Unveiled: A History of Modern Turkey*, which combines both serious scholarship with journalistic nosiness. It gives a good feel for both late Kemalism in action and the rise of Turkey's Islamist political parties. Graham E. Fuller's *The New Turkish Republic: Turkey as a Pivotal State in the Muslim World* should also be read, even though Mr. Fuller appears at times to be cheering on Turkey's movement away from America.

And on democracy in general, I have only one essential book—Samuel P. Huntington's *The Third Wave: Democratization in the Late Twentieth Century.*

ABOUT THE AUTHOR

Reuel Marc Gerecht, a former case officer in the CIA, is a senior fellow at the Foundation for Defense of Democracies. He is a contributing editor at *The Weekly Standard* and a contributing writer for *The New Republic*'s "Entanglements" page on foreign affairs. He is the author of *Know Thine Enemy: A Spy's Journey into Revolutionary Iran* and *The Islamic Paradox: Shiite Clerics, Sunni Fundamentalists, and the Coming of Arab Democracy*.

HERBERT AND JANE DWIGHT
WORKING GROUP ON
ISLAMISM AND THE
INTERNATIONAL ORDER

The Herbert and Jane Dwight Working Group on Islamism and the International Order seeks to engage in the task of reversing Islamic radicalism through reforming and strengthening the legitimate role of the state across the entire Muslim world. Efforts will draw on the intellectual resources of an array of scholars and practitioners from within the United States and abroad, to foster the pursuit of modernity, human flourishing, and the rule of law and reason in Islamic lands—developments that are critical to the very order of the international system.

The Working Group is chaired by Hoover fellows Fouad Ajami and Charles Hill with an active participation of Director John Raisian. Current core membership includes Russell A. Berman, Abbas Milani, and Shelby Steele, with contributions from Zeyno Baran, Reuel Marc Gerecht, Ziad Haider, John Hughes, Nibras Kazimi, Bernard Lewis, Habib C. Malik, Camille Pecastaing and Joshua Teitelbaum.

INDEX